THE BEGINNER'S GUIDE TO
COSPLAY
ARMOR & PROPS

Craft Epic Fantasy Costumes and Accessories with EVA Foam

JOYCE VAN DEN GOOR

Founder of Pretzl Cosplay

PAGE STREET
PUBLISHING CO.

DEDICATION

TO EVERYONE WHO HAS USED MY PATTERNS AND
TUTORIALS TO MAKE THEIR OWN DREAMS COME TRUE,
YOUR SUPPORT MAKES IT POSSIBLE FOR ME TO HAVE MY DREAM JOB.
SEEING WHAT YOU CREATE MAKES ME SMILE EVERY DAY.

PAGE STREET
PUBLISHING CO.

First published in 2023 by
Page Street Publishing Co.
27 Congress Street, Suite 1511
Salem, MA 01970
www.pagestreetpublishing.com

Distributed by Macmillan, sales in Canada by The Canadian Manda Group.

27 26 25 24 23   1 2 3 4 5

ISBN-13: 978-1-64567-814-4
ISBN-10: 1-64567-814-8

Library of Congress Control Number: 2022950260

Cover and book design by Laura Benton for Page Street Publishing Co.
Photography by Pascal Deguelle and Joyce van den Goor

Printed and bound in China

CONTENTS

INTRODUCTION

I have always been interested in fantasy worlds with magical creatures. If you ask my parents what I was doing when I was a little girl, they'll probably tell you I was drawing horses and imaginative worlds or creating various fantasy things like dragon sculptures and paintings.

Starting from a very young age, my vivid imagination helped me develop my creativity. Fantasy movies, books, video games and tabletop role-playing games sparked my interest for the genre even more and made me want to dress up like the characters I got to know from these mediums. On top of that, in the early 2000s, I was really into gothic fashion, and those clothes were quite hard to find in my hometown in the Netherlands, and also expensive. That's when I asked my mother to teach me how to sew and to create my own gothic dresses with some elvish fantasy flair. At first, I got a lot of help from her, who happily taught me how to work with fabrics and turn these materials into the outfits I had in my mind. Later, I kept experimenting with materials and techniques and made outfits for myself. I couldn't have been a prouder teenager when I wore my self-made fantasy costumes to local medieval fairs.

Over the years, I've used many different materials to not only make dresses, but to also experiment with crafting swords, daggers, crowns and even some armor . . . which all failed terribly. I regret not taking photos of those attempts before I threw them away because it would illustrate how making armor and props is a skill that develops over time through a lot of practice.

It was only around 2010 that I discovered cosplay. That opened a whole new world for me, because I realized cosplay is a hobby that's enjoyed worldwide. I kept creating fantasy outfits for the medieval fairs that were held yearly in the Netherlands, but I also started to look out for other events like comic-cons and anime-cons in the Netherlands and also across the border in Belgium and Germany. There was so much to explore! The inspiration for new costumes and props never ended.

I didn't just make costumes, but I also sewed fleece hats with cat ears or dragon spikes. In late 2014, I booked my first booth at a convention (FACTS, Belgium's largest comic-con) to sell my handmade hats. This was such a success that I started my creative business, Pretzl, in January 2015, and kept booking booths at conventions to sell more of my hats and eventually also hoodies with dragon wings and tails, all of which I made myself.

Endlessly inspired by all the cosplayers at the conventions, I made more and more costumes and also props for myself to wear, using Worbla-brand thermoplastics and EVA foam. I shared my endeavors on social media pages like Facebook and Instagram and received lots of questions from other crafters about how I approached different parts of the costume-making process. I was happy to answer, but with the quick growth of my following, the questions became plentiful, and it became difficult to answer them all. So, I decided to film some tutorial videos for YouTube and Instagram where I explained some techniques and showed how I created my projects. I also began to digitize the armor and prop patterns I created and made those available on Etsy and later on my own website as well.

Slowly, Pretzl became more focused on cosplay tutorials and digital printable patterns, and the fleece hats and hoodies took a backseat. (I still make and sell the hats and hoodies on my online stores though. I want to keep them there as a constant reminder of how it all started. I still truly love to create them.)

Creating costumes and props with foam is a lot of fun. And if I can do it, why wouldn't you be able to? In this book, I have compiled the most important things I know about working with EVA foam to help get you started. This material is great for use in cosplay armor and props because it's easily accessible in most parts of the world and also beginner friendly. Even though the EVA foam sheets are inexpensive, I know the materials and tools can add up. However, if you craft and store your armor and props carefully, they'll last for a very long time!

The hands-on tutorials are, in essence, beginner friendly and laid out in a way so they're easy to understand and put into practice. The armor pieces and props described in this book all have decorations and are shaped so they will work together to form full outfits. By simply changing the paint colors and mixing and matching different pieces, your costumes can look totally different from the ones in this book. Free your creativity and craft your dream armor and props!

I'm so happy and grateful this book landed in your hands. I hope it will be a precious resource you can use over and over again in your crafting journey. And why not read it multiple times? When you have progressed more and have gotten more advanced, you may even discover new things you didn't notice when you read the book the first time.

I believe cosplay is for everyone. Yes—also for you.

Happy crafting!

Jayce van den Goor

COSTUME IDEAS

The projects described in this book can all be made individually, but they also work great together to form full costumes.

Wood Elf—A Creature of the Forest

Deep in the forest, the wood elf with curved horns and long pointy ears is gathering herbs and mushrooms to bring home to the elven village, high up in the ancient trees. The forest houses many dangers, and the elf has honed the art of archery to survive. The armor, made with natural materials like bark, horns and leather, leaves plenty of room for movement so the elf can run swiftly through the forest.

PROJECTS NEEDED TO MAKE THIS COSTUME:

Curved Horns (page 47)

Enchanted Elven Ears (page 54)

Deadly Horned Pauldrons (page 59)

Layered Elven Bracers (page 83)

Corset Belt (page 121)

Layered Elven Greaves (page 131)

Elvish Bow, Quiver and Arrows (page 151)

Sorceress—A Wielder of Magic

Well versed in the arcane art of magic, this sorceress can cast spells and enchantments that are written in the ancient leather-bound tome. The beautifully decorated and elegant armor protects the sorceress in battles of magic. Could the gems on the armor be enchanted? Possibly . . .

PROJECTS NEEDED TO MAKE THIS COSTUME:

Royal Headpiece (page 37)

Noble Layered Pauldrons (page 64)

Dignified Bracers (page 90)

Magical Sorceress' Breastplate (page 105)

Regal Hip Armor (page 125)

Magic Spellbook (page 179)

Knight—A Brave Warrior

This brave warrior's armor looks finely crafted . . . like it's made by the best blacksmith in the kingdom. With this heavy steel plate armor, the noble knight is a sight to behold. Armed with a sword and shield, this brave warrior is afraid of nothing and is ready to protect the castle.

PROJECTS NEEDED TO MAKE THIS COSTUME:

Combat Helmet (page 42)

Battleworn Shoulder Armor and Gorget (page 72)

Heroic Heavy Arm Armor (page 95)

Epic Knight Gauntlets (page 101)

Knight Chestplate (page 114)

Gallant Heavy Leg Armor (page 137)

Silver Foot Armor (page 145)

Knight's Shining Sword (page 165)

Protective Shield (page 173)

PART I

AN INTRODUCTION TO FOAM

In this section, we'll take a close look at the various types and forms of EVA foam that you can use and the different tools that will help you turn the material into epic cosplay armor and props.

Types of Foam

One does not simply walk into a craft shop and ask for EVA foam. There are different types, shapes and sizes of foam that are important to know about before you go shopping for materials.

EVA foam mostly comes in sheets, and those can be small sample sizes or large sheets that are rolled up to make them transportable. A commonly found size of foam sheet is 24 x 60 inches (60 x 150 cm). But there's also foam clay and even premade foam shapes. The good news is that all of these options work together just fine. The projects in this book have recommendations on which types of foam to use for the different elements.

FOAM SHEETS

EVA foam comes in various thicknesses and densities. The density has to do with the weight of the foam. In the United States, most EVA foam sold for cosplay will be high-density foam, which is heavier, stiffer and has a smoother surface and smaller pores. Low-density foam is more lightweight, softer and has a more textured surface because the pores in the material are bigger. These distinctions are very hard to see with the naked eye, so you'll have to trust what's written on the package.

If a store has various densities available, you can compare them by feeling the sheets. You'll notice that you can press down on the low-density foam easier than the high-density foam. The low-density foam will also be easier to bend; therefore it is great to use for organic shapes like horns. High-density foam is less fragile, so it can be more useful for armor parts. However, if you want to create textures on the foam by, for example, burning lines in it with a woodburning tool, the low-density foam (despite being more fragile) can still be a good choice.

High- or low-density foam doesn't mean high or low quality. It's just the softness that changes, and both can be great for projects. You can even combine the two in one project. The best foam choice completely depends on the project you want to create and what's available.

Because low-density foam has bigger pores than high-density foam, it will suck up more primer and paint, and therefore, you'll possibly need to apply more layers of primer to it.

In Europe, we have both low-density and high-density foam options widely available, which makes certain techniques like burning texture and creating detailed organic shapes easier. However, in certain places, such as the United States, most foam that's sold will be high-density. That's why I don't include low-density foam in the material lists for the projects.

EVA foam sheets are available in various thicknesses, but there are some differences between the continents. Here in Europe, the most common thicknesses of foam are 2mm, 5mm and 10mm. In the United States, however, the most common sizes are 2mm, 4mm, 6mm and 10mm. There are more thicknesses available, like super-thin 1mm foam or even sheets thicker than 10mm.

The various densities and thicknesses of foam can be confusing, but there are some swaps that you can make if you can't find the exact foam I list in the projects. Especially with the density, if you can find low-density EVA foam, it will make some of the techniques in the book easier to do.

EVA foam sheets come in different colors, ranging from bright colors such as purple and yellow, to more neutral shades like white, gray and black. The color of foam you choose doesn't really matter, since you'll be painting it later anyway. For the projects in this book, I used different colors of foam so the detailing on the projects would be more visible on the step-by-step photographs.

Mentioned in the book	Substitute with
4mm high-density EVA foam	5mm low-density EVA foam
6mm high-density EVA foam	5mm high-density EVA foam

Foam Sheets

Foam Prefabs

Foam Clay

Note: If you can't find EVA foam sheets in your area, you can also use foam floor mats. It's the same material, but the downside is that one side of this foam will have a texture that may look bad on your armor. A solution is to use the foam with the textured side on the inside or to sand the texture off. I always recommend going with the smooth EVA foam sheets, but if you have no other option, the EVA floor mats will work too.

FOAM CLAY

Foam clay is sold in jars, and you can sculpt with it. Sculpting with foam clay can be done with your hands, but clay modeling tools can be a great help for creating beautiful details. When some water is added, foam clay will stick to EVA foam sheets, so you won't always need glue to adhere foam clay details to EVA foam armor or props.

Foam clay is available in different colors, but the color you choose doesn't really matter since you'll be painting it after it's cured. For the projects in this book, I used a medium gray foam clay so the step-by-step photographs would show a better contrast between the foam clay details and the light gray and black foam base.

FOAM PREFABS

EVA foam can be carved and sanded into shapes, but this can be tricky, and you may not always have enough time to do all that. When the convention is soon, we have to do all we can to speed up the cosplay crafting process. That's when these so-called foam prefabs come in handy. These are premade shapes made out of high-density EVA foam that you can glue on your foam projects. And they'll look perfect immediately. So easy and fast! It can get pricy if you need a lot of these, because EVA foam sheets are cheaper. But prefabs can save a lot of time, and they look super-neat, so they can definitely be worth it.

Foam prefabs come in various shapes and sizes. Most popular are the (half) dowels and bevels. These are round, triangular-shaped and even trapezoid-shaped. These work amazingly well for adding decorative edges to cosplay armor.

These prefabricated dowels and bevels are mostly sold in 36-inch (91-cm)-long pieces in the United States and 1 meter (39 inches) long in Europe. Diameters can range from super tiny 5mm up to 40mm, which is quite chunky. The most commonly used diameter is 10mm for both the half-round dowels and the triangular bevels.

Dowels and bevels are not the only shapes you can find as foam prefabs. There are also spheres, cones, (dragon) scales and even chain mail and scale mail that you can buy ready-made. I'm sure this range will be expanded even more in the future, so always keep your eyes open for interesting foam shapes to use in cosplay projects.

The foam prefabs are all made out of high-density EVA foam, and therefore they are bendable, squishy and light-weight. They can easily be cut with a craft knife, and the thin dowels can even be cut with a pair of scissors.

For the projects in this book, I used some foam half dowels and bevels in various sizes and shapes. The ones I used are all black, but they can be found in different colors too. Which color of foam prefabs you use doesn't matter because you'll be painting the pieces.

Tools and Materials

As a beginner, it can feel overwhelming to see so many tools listed, especially power tools. But the good news is that you might already have a lot of these handy because they're all regular household tools that are not specific to cosplay crafting.

For anything you don't have, if you're on a tight budget, I recommend choosing the cheaper versions of the tools first. Later on, you can decide if you love armor and prop making enough to invest in higher quality, more expensive tools. I started with cheaper versions too, and when they eventually broke down, I upgraded to more expensive, professional ones.

The tools you see here are based on my personal favorites, but they're not definite. If you find additional tools that you want to use, that's perfectly fine too!

Heat Gun and Silicone Mat

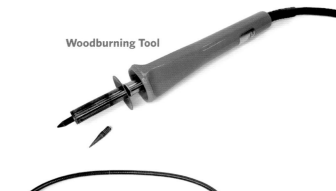

Woodburning Tool

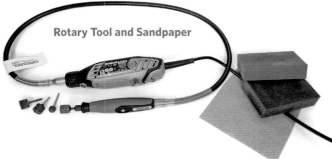

Rotary Tool and Sandpaper

Markers and Pens

Brushes, Sponges and Cloth

Knives and Cutting Mat

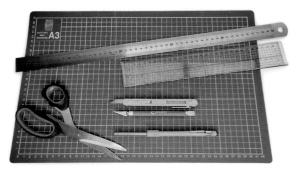

Cutters and Pliers

Reinforcement Materials

Elastic and D-rings for Straps

Primer

Sewing Machine

Paint

Varnish

Fillers

Glue

Masks and Protective Eyewear

PART II

CRAFTING WITH FOAM

Once you have some materials on hand and have a starter toolkit, you can begin with the real work: the crafting! Let's take a closer look at various techniques for building armor and props with foam, how to do detailing and how to finish all the hard work with a nice paint job that you can be proud of.

Safety Guidelines

Remember to always practice safety first and read the instruction manual you get with any tool to learn exactly how to use it properly. Here are a few other safety guidelines to keep in mind while working on the projects in this book.

Heat-shaping, heat-sealing and woodburning: While foam itself isn't toxic, it does give off toxic fumes when heated or melted. To protect your lungs from inhaling these fumes, wear a respirator that filters vapors and gasses while using a woodburning tool or heat gun on the foam.

Contact cement: Contact cement is toxic too, and can be irritating to the skin. Wear the respirator while gluing foam with contact cement, and prevent skin contact with the wet glue.

Spray paint or varnish: When using spray paint, it's preferable to work outside or in a well-ventilated area, and wear the respirator.

Sanding and rotary tools: When sanding foam with a rotary tool, wear long hair in a braid so it won't get caught in the swiftly rotating tool, and also wear a dust mask and safety goggles to prevent the sanded foam particles from getting in your lungs and eyes. Use a vacuum cleaner hose to suck up the foam dust while sanding.

Some of the tools used for foam crafting get really hot, so be careful not to touch the hot parts.

I keep a first aid kit, a fire extinguisher and a fire blanket on hand just in case of an emergency. Call me paranoid, but it can never hurt to have these things in the workshop.

Using the Templates

In the back of this book, you'll find folded pattern sheets that have the full-size templates for all of the larger pattern pieces. These templates are here to help you with crafting the projects. The rest of the templates will fit on regular printer paper and can be conveniently printed out. To download the printable templates, or if you have purchased the ebook edition of *The Beginner's Guide to Cosplay Armor & Props*, please use the link and password below:

Link: www.joycedesign.nl/beginnersguidetemplates
Password: 9781645678144

Don't throw the templates away so you can always refer back to them whenever you want to create another project from this book. To keep the pattern sheets intact, use other paper to trace and cut the templates you need, and put the original pattern sheets back in the book. Everything you need to know (e.g., how many times you need to cut the pieces, which thickness of foam you need, how you need to cut the foam and what project it is for) is written on the templates.

REGISTRATION MARKS

On every template, you'll notice little lines and other small shapes along the edges of the patterns. These are registration marks and are used to help you identify where the foam pieces need to be matched up while gluing them together. **Make sure to copy over any registration marks onto the foam with your paint marker when you are tracing your patterns.**

MIRRORING A TEMPLATE

Some pattern pieces need to be cut out of the foam once, but others might be needed multiple times or mirrored in order to create the whole object. To mirror a template, simply flip the template upside down and trace the new shape.

RESIZING A TEMPLATE

The templates are all drafted by me, so they are all in my size. Most of the projects are one-size-fits-all, but when a template needs to be adjusted to your own measurements, it's explained in the project's description.

There are several ways to resize a template. If a certain piece needs to be smaller or bigger, you can use a copier to make a copy at a percentage that is either lower or higher than 100 percent. This will make the end result smaller or bigger.

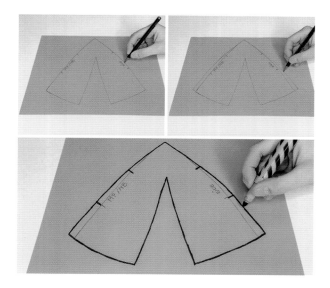

When cutting foam, knives will dull quickly. Therefore, it's important to sharpen your knives often! There are different types of tools available for sharpening knives, like whetstones or sharpening rods. My personal favorite is a pen-shaped sharpener that I simply run the blade of the knife across to give it a sharp edge again. A brand of knives that I really like is Excel Blades (from the United States). If you can't find any of these tools, simple sandpaper will work too. Just run the blade across the sandpaper to sharpen it.

How often it's necessary to sharpen the blade will depend on factors like the density and thickness of the foam and the lengths you will need to cut. It's always better to sharpen the blade too much rather than too little, since a dull blade will make ugly cuts in the foam, and those will be more work to clean up later on. Clean cuts in the foam will make it much easier to glue multiple pieces together with a nice and neat (sometimes nearly invisible if you do it really well!) glue seam. So don't skip the sharpening when you are cutting foam.

To protect your worktable, use a cutting mat. These come in various colors and sizes, so just pick one that fits on your worktable and is big enough for the pieces you want to cut. My go-to cutting mat is 16.5 x 12 inches (45 x 30 cm) (A3), but I also have a big one that's 33 x 23 inches (90 x 60 cm) (A1). The smaller one is easier to grab in-between working on a project, but the large one is perfect when I'm starting a new project and have many pattern pieces drawn out on the foam that I need to cut out.

When cutting the foam, make sure to hold the knife in a diagonal position toward the working surface. This will make cutting the material much easier and will result in a cleaner cut, which also takes less force from your hand.

Note: Of course, always be careful when using knives, and always cut away from yourself to prevent cutting yourself.

The angle of the cut is also very important and will determine how your finished piece looks when it's glued together. There are four basic types of cuts you can make in foam: straight cut, angled cut, varied cut and undercut. Let's take a close look at all four.

If you just want to narrow or widen an armor piece, you won't need to resize the full template, just the sides. First, determine how much narrower or wider the end result will need to be so it will fit you better, and then take away or add extra width on both sides of the template. Make sure that you take away or add the right amount. For example, if you need an extra 2 inches (5 cm) to make the helmet fit, check how many times you will need to cut the template piece out of foam first. You can add width to both sides of the template, and if the template needs to be cut out of the foam four times like with the helmet, that means that you will need to divide that original 2 inches (5 cm) by 8 (which accounts for both sides of each of the 4 foam pieces). Then add that smaller amount to both sides of the helmet base template. Also, move the registration marks to the new edges of the template, so you can still use them while gluing the foam pieces together.

Cutting

Cutting foam may seem simple, but it's a very important step that can make or break the final look of your project. Since foam is a soft material, it can be cut with simple tools like craft knives or box cutters. Thin foam (1mm to 2mm thick) can even be cut with household scissors.

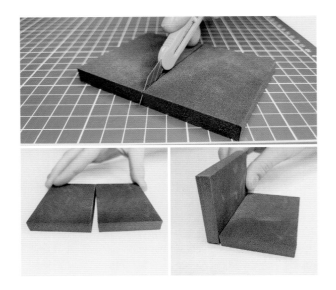

STRAIGHT CUT

Most cuts in foam will be straight cuts. Simply cut the foam how it feels most natural, and it will result in a straight, 90-degree angle. Try to keep your knife straight while cutting. If you don't have a very steady hand, a metal ruler can be a great help.

When gluing two pieces of foam that were cut like this together, it will result in a flat surface or a 90-degree corner if you quarter-turn one of the pieces.

ANGLED CUT

Another often-used cut is the angled cut. This is when you hold the knife at an angle when cutting the foam. This can be an inward or outward angle, depending on how you want your finished piece to look. Most of the time, an angled cut will be about 45 degrees, but it can also be a bit less or more.

When gluing two pieces of foam that were cut like this together, it will result in a more or less sharp corner (depending on the angle). The sharper the corner needs to be, the more angled the cut needs to be. These angled cuts can be really helpful for many foam projects, though it can be a bit tricky when you start out. Just try it out and get a feel for it, and you'll get better in no time!

VARIED CUT

Sometimes a straight or angled cut just . . . doesn't *cut* it, right? So, there's also the possibility to do a varied cut, where a part of the cut is straight and another part is angled. To make a cut like this, first decide which parts of the cut will need to be angled and which won't, and then simply change the angle of the blade gradually while you are making the cut. Try to do this in one go to make a nice clean cut in the foam.

This type of cut can be super useful for detailed organic shapes. For example, the Curved Horns (page 47) use varied cuts to prevent material bulking up at the tips and to make it easier to glue the tips together with a nice and pointy look. For most foam projects, however, you won't need this type of cut.

UNDERCUT

Another special and fun way to cut foam is the so called undercut, where the underside of the foam is cut. An undercut is made by cutting about 75 percent through the backside of the foam, either in a V-shaped cut where some material is taken out, or just a straight cut 75 percent through the foam.

After this cut is made, the foam can be folded closed or open, depending on which of the above you chose, resulting in a ridge or a ditch on the outside of the foam, without any glue seams showing.

When you want a ridge on the outside of the foam, make a V-shaped cut until about 75 percent into the back of the foam, and take the bit of foam away that you cut out (don't throw this away just yet though). Then add some contact cement inside the groove and fold it closed. Now on the outside, there is a neat-looking straight ridge.

When you want a ditch on the outside of the foam, make a straight cut about 75 percent into the back of the foam, fold this open and apply a bit of contact cement inside it. Take the bit of material that you cut away from the V-shaped cut that we made earlier and press it in the opened fold when the glue starts to dry. Now, on the outside, there is a neat-looking straight ditch.

This is a rather advanced method of cutting foam, but it can create such nice results in your final pieces. In this book, we're using the undercut technique in the Battleworn Shoulder Armor and Gorget (page 72) and the Gallant Heavy Leg Armor (page 137).

Note: Take the mentioned angles and depths of the cuts with a grain of salt. These are meant to illustrate the general idea of the different types of cuts in foam. It's OK if your angled cut is not perfectly 45 degrees, for example. Foam is a soft material, so there is definitely some wiggle room here because you can mostly still force it into the right shape while gluing everything together. I personally never calculate the angles, but always wing it . . . and it always works. If you cut two pieces of foam and hold them together to see how the total piece would look if you glued them together, and then notice that the angle was not quite right, you can still sand the edges of the foam with a rotary tool or sandpaper to get it to the right angle. So, don't worry; it will be alright.

Gluing

The best glue for EVA foam is contact cement. This is a really strong glue, and it can be found in tubes (gel) and cans (liquid). I mostly use DuraColl from Minque in the Netherlands or contact cement from Cosplayshop Select Style in Belgium. Good alternatives are Barge, Weldwood, Pattex and Bison contact cements. Before opening the can, it's important to know how to properly use this adhesive to get the most out of it.

USING A SQUEEZE BOTTLE FOR MORE CONVENIENT USE

To make the glue easier to use, I recommend taking a small plastic squeeze bottle (mine is 2 ounces [60 ml]) and squeezing some contact cement inside it. Remember to close the can of glue immediately so that it doesn't dry out. The glue will also dry out in the plastic squeeze bottle, but it will take a couple of days or up to a week. I find that using a squeeze bottle makes it much more convenient to apply the glue directly onto your foam projects and can help prevent wasting materials. Just suck up as much glue into the bottle as you think you'll need that day and the next, and put more from the can into the bottle when it's empty.

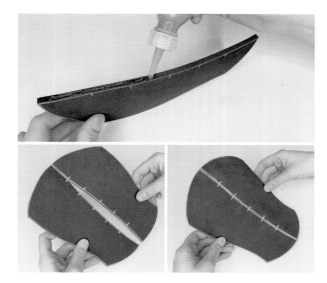

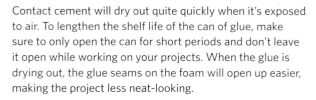

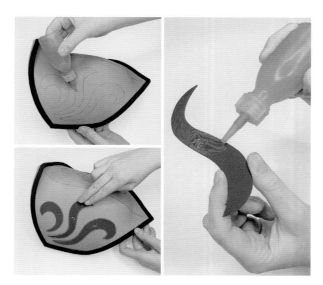

Contact cement will dry out quite quickly when it's exposed to air. To lengthen the shelf life of the can of glue, make sure to only open the can for short periods and don't leave it open while working on your projects. When the glue is drying out, the glue seams on the foam will open up easier, making the project less neat-looking.

GLUING FOAM TOGETHER

Use the squeeze bottle to apply some contact cement on both pieces of foam that you want to glue together and spread it out in a thin layer using a scrap piece of foam or a spatula. Let the glue air-dry for a few minutes, or until it's not wet anymore but tacky. You can see the texture of the glue change from glossy (wet) to matte (dry enough). This usually only takes a few minutes, but the exact time might vary depending on your local climate and the brand of glue.

When the glue is dry enough, take the two pieces of foam and press them firmly together to form a really strong bond. The glue sticks immediately, so do your best to get the two pieces together correctly immediately because you won't get a second try. However, if a glue seam is not super clean, don't worry. You can still sand it smooth after the glue has fully dried (a few hours later, or even better, overnight).

Note: In the templates in this book, you will see little lines and shapes like triangles or half circles printed along the edges of the pattern pieces. These are registration marks designed so that you know exactly where to align two pieces of foam while gluing them together. On some pattern pieces, like the Curved Horns (page 47), it may look like the registration marks don't align. Trust the marks, and force the foam a bit while gluing them together to make the registration marks align. This will allow for nice organic (sometimes curled) shapes to form.

Foam pieces will need to be glued together to form bigger three-dimensional shapes like armor pieces, but you'll also want to glue layers onto the foam to create details and edging. When adding layers of details to the foam, just use the same method and apply a thin layer of contact cement to both the foam (armor) piece and the detail piece, and then press the two together after the contact cement has become tacky.

Note: Safety first. Contact cement is toxic and the fumes are not healthy to inhale. So, always work in a well-ventilated area and wear a respirator mask that protects your lungs from vapors and gasses. Prevent skin contact with the wet contact cement. Using a squeeze bottle to apply the glue, and a little scrap piece of foam to spread it out, will help prevent the glue from touching your skin.

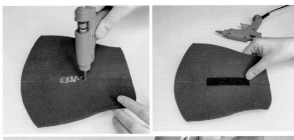

Sanding

You can sand foam to shape your piece, smooth edges or correct glue seams that weren't made perfectly even. Power sanding tools like a rotary tool, delta sander (or detail sander) or even a belt sander are great for this purpose. I prefer to use a rotary tool for sanding foam. However, a rotary tool can be heavy to hold, so to make it easier, I advise using a flex shaft with it. This is an extended piece that can be attached to the tip of the rotary tool. It is lighter than the rotary tool and much more ergonomic to hold while sanding foam.

While you are sanding foam, always keep a vacuum cleaner running to suck up most of the dust that comes off.

Pro Tip: When I use my rotary tool, I put the tool on my table on top of a folded towel to absorb the vibrations of the tool. It's also possible to hang the tool on a dedicated stand when using it, although it depends on the brand of rotary tool you use, whether or not this is recommended. Always read the instruction manual to learn exactly how to use your tools properly and safely.

When first using your rotary tool, play around a little bit with the different speed settings and various bits that can be placed on it like sanding drums and grinding bits. I mostly use the 60-grit and 120-grit sanding drums for sanding foam and creating battle damage. The rougher 60-grit sanding drum is perfect for sanding larger pieces of foam and getting it into the basic shape you want. To smooth the surface, the finer 120-grit sanding drum works best. For creating interesting textures on the foam (like hammered metal), the stone grinding bits are very useful.

The speed in which the tool rotates will determine how the surface of the foam will look when you use it. Too slow and it won't work very well; too fast, and it may take away too much material too quickly.

OTHER GLUES

Another type of glue that will come in handy when working with foam is hot glue. It won't work very well for gluing pieces of foam together neatly because it's rather difficult to make an invisible glue seam with this type of glue. But hot glue works like a charm for gluing strips of Velcro® fastener to the inside of a foam armor piece to make attachments. To add a piece of Velcro to foam, first apply some hot glue on the foam where the Velcro needs to go and press the piece of Velcro firmly on while the glue is still fluid. Then apply some additional hot glue around the whole edge of the piece of Velcro, making sure to cover the edge so it will stay put.

When making straps and attachments for armor pieces, fabric glue is also useful.

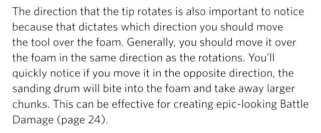

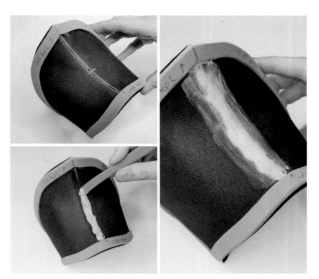

The direction that the tip rotates is also important to notice because that dictates which direction you should move the tool over the foam. Generally, you should move it over the foam in the same direction as the rotations. You'll quickly notice if you move it in the opposite direction, the sanding drum will bite into the foam and take away larger chunks. This can be effective for creating epic-looking Battle Damage (page 24).

If you are on a budget, you can also choose to use sandpaper or sanding sponges. The result won't be as smooth as with power tools, but it will still work. You can also sand foam clay! Just be sure to wait until the foam clay is fully cured, which usually takes a couple of days, depending on the thickness of the sculpt.

Filling Gaps and Seams

If a glue seam ends up looking messy, and sanding doesn't completely smooth it out, there are always fillers that can come to the rescue!

A well-known and easy-to-find filler is DAP® Kwik Seal®, which is a thick paste of acrylic latex caulk that can be spread on the foam with a spatula and left to air-dry. There are also fillers that are specifically designed for cosplay crafting available at cosplay stores. It doesn't matter which one you use, since they all work. My personal favorite is Craft Filler by Poly-Props in the U.K. DAP Kwik Seal is the easiest to find in the United States.

To fix a seam, take your filler of choice and apply it with a spatula onto the seam that you want to hide. Add some water to it and smooth it out with your fingers. Some fillers may require you to wear gloves for touching it, so always read the packaging.

Put the project aside to dry overnight. The next day, the filler will be fully cured and ready for sanding. You can also add another layer of filler, if the first layer didn't cover the gaps completely.

Pro Tip: If you really can't seem to get rid of an ugly glue seam, then just call it battle damage. You could even add more battle damage by sanding some material away to make it look like you planned it like that all along.

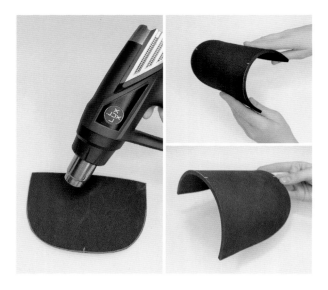

Heat-Shaping

EVA foam sheets are originally flat, but they can be shaped with heat. For this, you will need a heat gun. Heat guns are power tools and are sold by various brands. It doesn't really matter which brand you pick because most of them will be just fine for the purpose of heating up EVA foam. My own heat gun has a variable temperature of 122 to 1130°F (50 to 610°C), but I never use the highest setting. In my experience, the sweet spot is around 572°F (300°C). Of course, that's already very hot, so never have the tool running for long periods at a time, and when you stop using it, remember to switch it off and put it aside where no one can trip over it or touch the metal tip, which stays really hot for quite some time after using it. It's better to be safe than sorry with so much heat. To protect your worktable from all that heat, use a silicone mat.

Heat the EVA foam by blowing hot air over it with a heat gun (I use it on 572°F [300°C]) and bend the foam into the shape you want while it's still warm. Make sure it cools down while in that shape by holding it for several minutes. After the material has cooled down, it will now hold its new shape. Sometimes you need to repeat the heat shaping. If a curve is not strong enough after cooling down, simply heat

the foam again and shape it further. Be careful not to burn and damage the foam though. All you are doing is warming it up. Always be careful not to blow the hot air on your fingers, and don't touch the hot parts of the tool.

Pro Tip: If you need a simple curve in the foam, you don't necessarily need to apply heat to shape it. It's also possible to take another layer of foam and glue both parts together while bending the foam. That way, the second layer of foam will help keep the curve in shape. This can be very helpful when you need a large curve, like in the Protective Shield (page 173).

Adding Texture

There are many ways to add texture to super smooth EVA foam. Some common techniques include stamping, sanding and burning textures into the material. Here are some techniques I use to recreate some of my favorite textures.

LEATHER

With a ball of rolled-up aluminum foil, you can create a leather-like texture on foam by simply pressing it on foam that's been heated up with a heat gun. Or, crinkle a piece of aluminum foil and press it with an iron (no steam), to cover larger surfaces. This texture will disappear if the foam is reheated, so if you want to use this technique, you'll need to plan accordingly.

HAMMERED METAL

With the stone-grinding bits on the rotary tool, you can create a texture that looks like hammered metal by simply sanding little round dents in the foam all over the surface.

BATTLE DAMAGE

The sanding drums that you can mount on the rotary tool will come in handy for creating textures like epic battle damage. Using the rotary tool with 120-grit sanding drum, sand some lines and dents into the outside of the project. Think

about where weapons could have touched the armor piece or prop and recreate slashes and cracks there. Make deeper and narrower lines to get more variation and texture. Don't work neatly while doing this, but make it messy so it looks realistic. Move the rotary tool over the foam in the opposite direction of the rotation to make the battle damage look even more gnarly. After the sanding is done, clean the foam piece by removing all of the dust. If you don't have a rotary tool, you can also create battle damage with a woodburning tool or soldering iron.

WOOD GRAIN

Using a woodburning tool or soldering iron, you can create a wood grain texture on foam. Because it's used to melt the foam, don't use an expensive soldering iron that you also use for actual soldering. Instead, pick an old one or get a cheap one that you can dedicate to burning foam. To create a wood grain texture, turn on your soldering iron or wood-burning tool and when it's heated up, simply start burning lines into the foam to create the texture. Press harder to create deeper, thicker lines or gentler for narrower, thinner lines. Of course, you can create other textures too.

Note: To protect your worktable when burning foam with a soldering iron or woodburning tool, put something over the surface, like a piece of wood or thick cardboard.

Be creative and find many ways to create awesome textures on your foam projects.

Adding Bevels

Edges on cosplay armor pieces are often decorated with bevels; however, you can also use bevels to create details like swirly lines on the armor pieces themselves. Bevels can have various shapes such as round, triangular or square, and they can be various thicknesses and widths too.

For a quick and easy way to add bevels, use EVA foam prefabs.

For a more cost-effective option, create your own bevels with EVA foam. Take a piece of foam that's the thickness you want for the bevel. Decide how wide you want the bevels to be, and mark lines on the foam. Then cut out long strips using a metal ruler to help get super straight cuts.

For square bevels: Your work is already done. Go ahead and glue them onto your foam project now.

For rounded bevels: Sand away some material on the edges. You can do that before gluing it to the armor piece, or afterward. But always keep in mind that you still need to be able to reach all the edges with the rotary tool. So that's why sometimes it can be better to sand the bevel into shape before gluing it on the armor piece.

For triangular bevels: Try to cut the strips of foam at an angle so the bevel will be in the desired shape already. You can always clean up the shape by sanding the foam afterwards.

Note: When adding a bevel on a curved shape, you don't actually need to cut the bevel in that shape. Bevels are thin enough to follow curved lines, so simply use a straight bevel and glue it curved along the piece.

Detailing with Foam Clay

Foam clay can be used to create textures and details on foam projects. It's super lightweight when it's cured, and with some water, it can stick to EVA foam. Because foam clay sticks to many surfaces, it's a good idea to use a silicone mat as a work surface for sculpting. Foam clay doesn't stick to silicone.

To start adding details on your project with foam clay, first add a bit of water to the EVA foam, put the foam clay where you want it and press it down. Most of the time, the water will be enough to adhere the clay to the foam. But if your details fall off the foam after the clay has cured, simply glue it down with some contact cement.

Foam clay can be molded with your hands or with the help of (wooden) clay modeling tools. Many different details can be formed this way. In this book, we'll use foam clay to create leaf details, faux gems and texture for horns.

Not all foam clay is identical. Some are drier, while others are wetter. When the clay is too dry, simply mix some water into it while kneading. This will make it smoother and easier to form small details. If the clay is too wet, leave it to air-dry until it feels better to work with. All of this is personal preference of course, so just try it out and feel what consistency you like to work with.

Foam clay air-dries. Any details that you make with this material will need 1 to 2 days to cure before you can paint them. Like I mentioned before, the consistency of foam clay brands varies, so when the clay cures, it may either shrink or expand a little bit. So, before making your final project, it's always a good idea to sculpt a little test piece, let it cure for a few days and decide if you like how the clay cured. You may need to adjust your sculpting process when you notice how the shape has changed after curing.

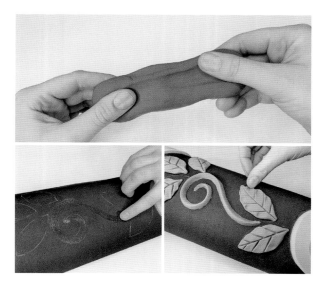

Because the clay air-dries, it's very important to keep it in a closed container. Most foam clays come double-sealed in a resealable plastic bag inside a jar with a lid. Always close the bag and the lid after taking out the clay you need.

When foam clay is fully cured (depending on the size of your project and your local climate, this can take multiple days), you can sand it with sandpaper to adjust the shape.

Heat-Sealing

After all the crafting, shaping and detailing, your project is done. Or is it? Before it can be painted, there's still one important step, and that's heat-sealing. Foam has pores, which will suck up primer and paint. By blowing heat on the foam with a heat gun, the pores will close, making the surface even flatter. The foam doesn't need a lot of heat, and you'll see it changing colors a bit while applying the heat to it. The foam project will take primer and paint much better after it is heat-sealed.

Make sure not to heat the foam up too much because you could burn the material. Also keep in mind that when the foam is warm, it can be shaped again. Keep the foam piece in the desired shape while it cools down, so it will hold its shape. If you created a texture in the foam by stamping (leather texture, for example), you won't need to heat it again to heat-seal it. If you do, you'll remove your stamped textures.

Priming, Painting and Protecting

When you are happy with how your foam project looks, it's time to prime, paint and then protect the paint job.

For applying primer, paint and varnishes, I like to use a combination of brushes and sponges. The brushes that I like most are makeup brushes. These often have soft bristles to prevent lots of visible brushstrokes, and the handles are not too long, making them comfortable to hold. They don't need to be expensive brushes at all. I personally love the brand Essence, which makes super-affordable makeup brushes.

Some brushes I keep as neat as possible so I can paint fine lines or big surfaces with them. But other brushes are used for dry brushing, which will kind of destroy the brushes. For the dry bushing technique, where you dab the paint on instead of swiping it on, this is exactly what you want! So definitely keep those brushes too and don't throw them away. Most primer and paints can be washed off the brushes with warm water and soap. For some paints though, a special brush cleaner can be useful.

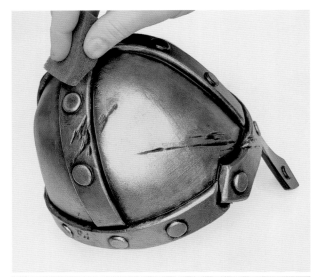

When I want a surface without any brushstrokes, I like to dab on the paint with sponges. This method is really effective with metallics. The sponges can be cleaned with warm water and soap, or just leave the paint on them, and then cut off the painted part later with some scissors.

Pro Tip: Instead of buying sponges, I like to repurpose materials used from packaging or use leftover pieces of upholstery foam from other cosplay projects. I just store them and cut them up when I want to use them for painting.

For applying waxy paints like Rub 'n Buff®, it's useful to use an old piece of cloth.

PRIMING

EVA foam needs to be primed first. Since foam is a material that stays flexible, it's important to use primers that are flexible too. There are primers that come in spray cans and primers that need to be applied with a brush.

A very well-known brand of flexible spray primer (and paint) is Plasti Dip®. It can be quite expensive though, since you can easily use multiple cans on one single armor and prop project. Other brands have recently come up with flexible primers especially designed for foam. Some of these may be more affordable. Spray-on products will be faster to use, but I feel like the brush-on products give me more control over my work.

An often-used flexible brush-on primer is FlexBond®, which is also used as a glue. It's easy to apply with a brush and dries translucent. There are also flexible brush-on primers that already have a color added to them. Some examples are HexFlex™ and Flexipaint.

Of all of these, black HexFlex is my ultimate favorite. It gives a nice, non-sticky, matte surface and air-dries, like all of these primers. The black color also really helps with painting, since it's a nice shadow color.

Choose the primer that you want to use (spray or brush-on) and apply it on the foam piece in thin layers. Leave the piece to air-dry for 2 to 4 hours in-between the layers of primer. When using a brush to apply primer, use as few brush-strokes as possible to get a super-smooth result.

When you apply primer, always paint the whole outside of the piece, and also a bit of the inside. If the armor piece will be worn directly against your body/clothes, a 1-inch (2.5-cm)-wide perimeter should be enough to cover the inside. But if the underside of the armor piece will be visible while wearing it, then make sure to prime anything that will be visible. Otherwise, the color of the raw foam will show when wearing the costume.

One layer of primer usually isn't enough to get a nice surface. I like to apply two or three layers of primer on a foam piece, but you can keep adding layers until you like how the surface looks. Then leave the primed piece to dry for 2 to 4 hours before continuing with the paint.

PAINTING

After the foam has been primed, you can use nearly any paint. Just keep in mind that paints will vary in flexibility after they've dried so make sure you check the container. If you use paint that's not flexible, it can cause cracks when wearing the armor.

While priming is pretty straightforward, painting can have more steps. Mostly you'll want to add a base color first, then add color over it and, optionally, add highlights and shadows to make the details *pop* even more.

You can use normal acrylic paint on primed EVA foam, but there are also paints specifically designed to be used on foam, which you can find at cosplay stores. Some examples of brush-on flexible paints are HexFlex, Flexipaint and Cospaint®. Some of these even come in wonderful metallic colors.

If looking for metallics, gilding waxes are an interesting option. Well-known brands are Rub 'n Buff and Pebeo Gilding Wax. These products are waxy and smell a bit like shoeshine. They produce an amazing metallic effect on foam.

Just like with the primer, you can also use spray paints. I've found though, that acrylic spray paints sometimes end up cracking when they dry. I don't know why this happens, but it's something to take note of. Plasti Dip also has colored sprays, so you can use those too. Here again, I prefer to use the brush-on paints and apply them either with brushes or sponges, depending on the effect I want.

With paint, there's so much to explore! Try some out, and discover which are your favorites. I don't have one favorite brand; I use a collection of many different ones I have gathered over time.

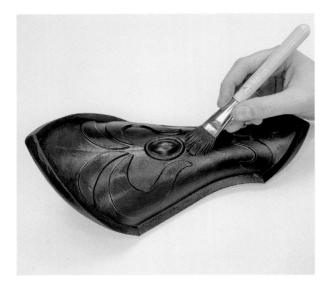

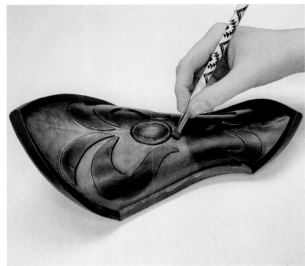

BASE COLOR

If you use a colored primer, for example black HexFlex, you can probably skip the step of adding a base color. But if the primer is uncolored, or if it has the wrong color, take some (acrylic) paint and apply it on the foam project everywhere that you put primer (which should include anywhere that will be visible when you wear it).

For the base color I like to use either black or brown. Black works great for cool colors like silver, and brown is good for warm colors like gold. For example: On the image above, I used black HexFlex as a primer, but I wanted the base color to be brown to get a warm undertone. So I added a layer of brown paint over the black. Of course, the base color you choose is completely up to you, and some interesting combinations can be made! So, by all means, experiment with color.

Most of the time, one layer of base color is enough, but if your paint has bad coverage, just apply multiple coats.

MAIN COLOR

When the base color is dry, apply the color of choice with your preferred tool: brush, sponge or spray can. There are no rules as to when you should use a brush and when you should use a sponge. It's mainly personal preference, and you can find out what works best for you by experimenting. Different paint brands and sometimes even different colors will work better with different tools.

Whichever tool you use to apply the paint, and how you handle that tool, will change how the painted surface looks. You can experiment with different tools and movements for different effects. Here are some examples:

- When you use the brush to make long, even brushstrokes you can add a covering layer of paint onto an area, but it will leave brushstrokes on the final piece.

- When dabbing paint on with either a brush or sponge, there won't be any brushstrokes.

- If you use just a bit of paint on the brush while making these dabbing movements or stroking over the project, it's called dry brushing, and nice gradients can be made with this technique.

- Another option is to use an old piece of cloth to apply the paint. This works especially well with wax paints like Rub 'n Buff and other gilding waxes.

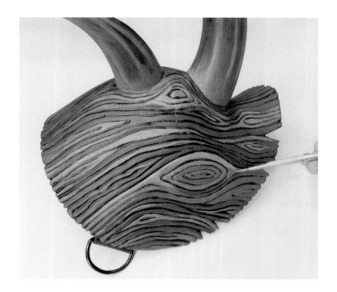

Most times, one layer won't be enough to get a full coverage with the color, so you'll want to apply multiple layers. Just remember to wait 2 to 4 hours for the last layer of paint to dry before adding the next.

Pro Tip: To get instant highlights and shadows, don't paint the exact same surface with the second layer of paint— just the parts that need to stand out more.

HIGHLIGHTS AND SHADOWS

You can use highlights and shadows to add more depth to your paint job. These are optional, but they can take your project to the next level.

Highlights: To make raised details stand out more, you can mix a lighter version of your main color by combining that color with some white paint. Use that new color to paint over only the raised parts. This gives your project some nice depth because the black (from the primer or base color) inside the texture lines will look like shadows. You can build up the highlights even more by mixing a lighter shade for each additional layer of highlights.

Pro Tip: To highlight a metallic color like gold, you can paint stripes of silver on the gold where you want to add (the illusion) of three-dimensionality.

Shadows: To create shadows, either mix a darker version of your main color or use black paint. Oil paint is great for shading because it has a really long drying time, and therefore it will stay wet and workable for much longer than acrylic paint. However, the long drying time can be a downside too, because it will take a long time before the paint is totally dry to the touch. Where I live, it takes more than a week for oil paint to dry, while acrylic paint takes less than a day.

Adding gradient shadows with oil paint can take the paint job to the next level. Apply some black oil paint to the edges on the piece that could use some shadows. Apply it with a thin brush first and then, with a larger, fluffier brush, blend the still wet paint out in a nice gradient.

Protecting

Once the paint is dry, you can add an optional varnish layer to protect your work so that your armor or prop will stay in better shape for longer. Depending on which type of finisher you use, it can add a special glossy, satin or matte effect to the whole project.

TYPES OF VARNISHES

Varnishes come both in spray cans and as brush-on products. Most of them don't dry completely flexible, so note that using it can take away some flexibility from the foam piece . . . but it's not always noticeable. There are spray finishers designed specifically for foam projects that do stay flexible, but I don't use these very often because I think they make the surface feel a bit rubbery.

Brush varnishes tend to be more beginner friendly because they're applied slowly, which gives you more control and less chance to get drips on the project. They're also especially helpful if you want to use multiple types of varnish on the same project. It's very important that you wait for everything to dry before applying brush-on varnishes so that you don't smear the paint job. Examples are: HexFlex Clear (flexible) and acrylic brush-on varnishes (semi-flexible).

Spray can varnishes are super quick, which make them useful for tighter deadlines. If you applied oil paint shadows, I also recommend you use spray varnish because you can use it before the oil paint fully dries (which can take weeks), and you're less likely to smear the paint job. Examples are: Valour Clear Coat from Poly-Props (flexible) and acrylic spray varnish (semi-flexible).

Pro Tip: If you plan on doing cosplay photoshoots with your armor and props, I recommend a satin finish. A super glossy finish can cause some flashback with studio lights, but the satin finish doesn't have that effect as much, and therefore more details of the paint job will stay visible in the final photographs.

If you want the piece to be super glossy, then a varnish with a glossy finish will add some extra shine to your work.

A project that shouldn't look like it's made out of metal can keep its matte look by applying a matte varnish over it. This is a great option for wood grain textured pieces or items that need to look like organic material.

You don't have to cover the full project in the same varnish. On some of the projects in this book, I used two different types of varnish. That made it possible to coat the main piece in matte varnish for example and paint details like faux gems or golden leaves with shiny, glossy varnish to make them look more realistic. To avoid getting the glossy varnish on the whole project, use a brush-on varnish instead of a spray varnish for this job.

TYPES OF FINISHES

Varnishes come in various finishes, ranging from matte to super glossy. For most armor and prop projects, I prefer a satin finish, which is between matte and glossy. For pieces that are painted in metallic colors, the satin finish will keep the shine but doesn't make it glossier than it really is.

Situation	Recommended type of varnish	Brush-on	Spray
Foam with tree bark texture	Matte	X	X
Horns (organic texture)	Matte	X	X
Foam that needs to look like leather	Matte	X	X
Realistically painted metallic armor	Satin	X	X
Armor with oil paint shading	Satin		X
Metallic armor that needs to be extra shiny	Glossy	X	X
Faux gems made with Foam clay	Glossy	X	
Sculpted leaves painted to look like metal	Glossy	X	

PART III

THE PROJECTS

Ready to get started for real and be done with the basics? This book contains 22 projects, complete with templates, for you to create some epic costumes and props for yourself! The projects are divided into groups, based on which body part they will be worn on. You can choose to craft one of the three main looks: the Knight, the Sorceress or the Wood Elf, but you can also choose to mix and match the projects and make a totally unique costume. The projects are designed to have versatile shapes, which you can also use (with some optional alterations and creativity) for your very own costume designs. Perhaps you want to make a costume based on your favorite video game character or a character from a book that you are reading. Just take inspiration from the projects in this book and craft your own amazing costumes with what you've learned.

MATERIALS

Royal Headpiece templates (pattern sheet I)

1 (14 x 14-inch [35 x 35-cm]) sheet of 6mm EVA foam

1 (4 x 4-inch [10 x 10-cm]) piece of 2mm EVA foam

79 inches (2 m) of EVA foam prefab triangular bevel (I used 10mm wide, low profile)

Contact cement

Foam clay

6 inches (15 cm) of EVA foam prefab half-round dowel (I used 5mm wide)

Painter's tape or duct tape

Flexible primer (black)

Acrylic paint (dark brown, metallic purple, pearl, gold and silver)

Black oil paint (optional)

Satin and glossy (spray) varnish (optional)

TOOLS

Measuring tape

Paint marker

Craft knife

Cutting mat

Heat gun

Safety tools, including a respirator, dust mask and safety glasses (review page 16)

Rotary tool with sanding drum (120-grit), or regular sandpaper

Wooden clay modeling tool (optional)

Brushes, for painting

ROYAL HEADPIECE
With Shining Gemstone

This elegant headpiece with pointy edges looks magnificent on a magical character such as a Sorceress or other spellcaster. The band that's attached on the back of this headpiece will keep it firmly on your head in a convenient way without adding much weight to this already super lightweight piece. The headpiece can be worn over your normal hair or over a wig and doesn't require hair clips or fasteners. It's really comfy! A beautiful gem is the shining center of this headpiece. It's not a real gem, but sculpted with foam clay instead. The painting and finishing make this gem look so realistic. The edges of the headpiece are decorated with triangular-shaped prefab EVA foam bevels to help speed up the crafting process.

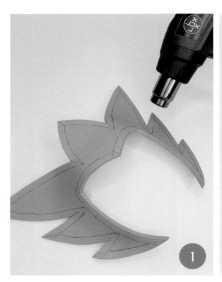

PREPARATION

Before cutting the foam, hold the cut-out paper template of the headpiece base to your head where you want to wear it. Using a tape measure, measure around the back of your head, between the markings on the template and add 2 inches (5 cm) to this measurement. This measurement will determine what length the EVA foam strap needs to be for making the headpiece wearable.

Once you know the measurement for your strap, cut a ¾-inch (2-cm)-wide piece of 6mm EVA foam to that length. For reference, mine was 14 inches (35 cm) long.

Using the paper pattern, trace and cut the headpiece base out of the 6mm EVA foam. Cut out the swirly details twice (once mirrored) using the 2mm EVA foam.

SHAPING THE HEADPIECE BASE

1. Heat the foam headpiece base with the heat gun. When the foam is hot, you can shape it to be rounded so that it will fit well on your forehead. Curve the foam piece and hold it for a few minutes in the desired shape until it's cooled down. Bend the pointy edges in the other direction to make them stand out to the sides more if you like how that looks. When the foam has cooled down again, you can try it on your head to see if you like the shape.

The sides of the headpiece should sit snug against your cheeks. If the shape isn't right just yet, heat the foam again and shape it further. Read more about heat shaping foam on page 24. If you want to keep it simple and don't want to add edging and details, move on to step 5 next and then skip the faux gemstone too.

ADDING DETAILS

2. Lay the triangular-shaped bevel along the edges of the headpiece to measure how long they should be, and cut to the right lengths. In order to achieve nice pointy corners, make sure to cut the ends diagonally. You should end up with 18 pieces.

Note: Each piece will vary in length, so to avoid mixing them up, write numbers or letters on them and on the corresponding part of the armor pieces where they need to go.

3. Glue the bevels all around the edge on the headpiece base using the contact cement. Where two pieces of bevel meet, glue these sides together so it forms one continuous bevel.

4. Take the two swirly detail pieces and glue those on both of the "ears" of the headpiece.

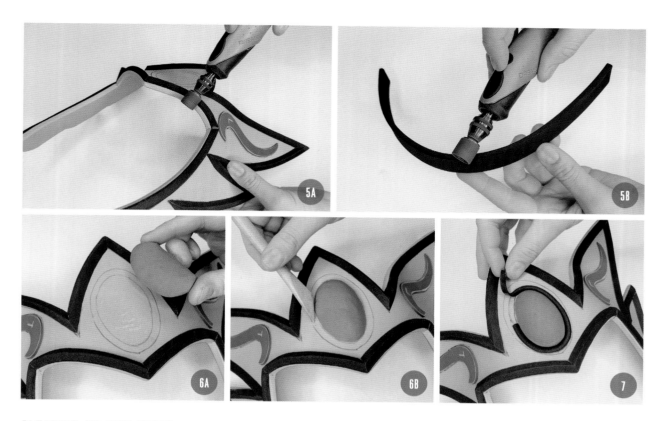

CLEANING UP THE EDGES

5. Using the rotary tool with 120-grit sanding drum, sand the edges of the headpiece smooth. The transition between the glued-on bevels and the headpiece will get super smooth in this step. Also sand the edges smooth of the strip of foam that will be used for the headband to make it softer. The result of the sanding will look nicest when using a rotary tool, but you can also use regular sandpaper for this job. After the sanding is done, clean the foam piece by removing all of the dust.

CREATING A FAUX GEMSTONE

6. Form a flat oval shape with a bit of foam clay. If the foam clay is too dry, mix some water into it. Using your fingers, apply a little bit of water on the armor where you want to place the gem. This will make the foam clay stick better to the foam.

Press the foam clay oval shape softly onto the base and push the clay's sides down until it is a cabochon shape. Use your fingers to do the sculpting and, optionally, some (wooden) clay modeling tools. Now set the project aside for 24 to 48 hours so the foam clay can air-dry. It doesn't matter if your gem isn't perfectly shaped right now, since it will get a bit puffier once the foam clay has air-dried.

7. Lay the half-round foam dowel around the cured foam clay gem, and cut it to the right length. Glue the dowel to the armor around the faux gem to create a gemstone setting. Also glue the sides where the two ends of the bevel meet to create one continuous bevel.

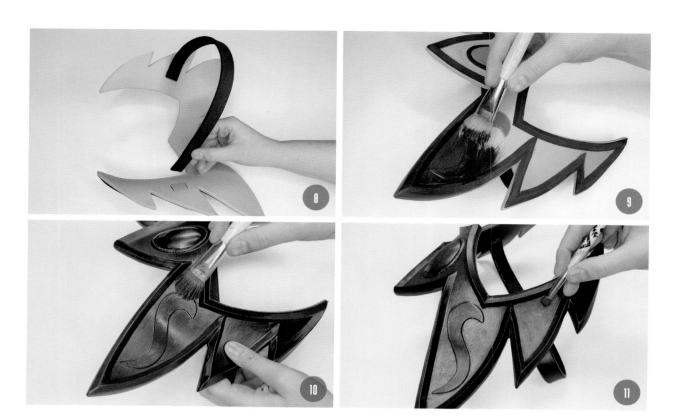

MAKE IT WEARABLE

8. Heat the thin EVA foam strap with the heat gun. When the foam strip is hot, you can shape it to be rounded and fit well on the back of your head. This piece will be the strap that keeps the headpiece snug on your head.

To decide where to glue the ends of this strap to the headpiece, try taping the strap to different spots on the backside and adjusting the length as needed until it sits perfectly on your head. Now take it off and mark where the strap needs to be attached. Glue both ends of the strap to the backside of the headpiece. Now the headpiece is wearable!

PRIMING AND PAINTING

9. Prepare the headpiece for priming and painting by heat-sealing it with the heat gun. Try to avoid heating the foam clay as much as possible, since it can get damaged.

When the foam is cool, apply the black flexible primer (page 27) to the headpiece. Cover the complete front of the piece and most of the back too. You can leave the parts that will be sitting against your skin (forehead) unprimed for comfort reasons. Also prime the outside of the strap on the back. Use as many coats of primer as needed until you like how the surface looks. I used two layers of HexFlex black. Leave the primer to dry for 2 to 4 hours.

10. Apply a layer of brown acrylic paint to the armor piece and headstrap. This will serve as the shadow color for the purple and gold paint. To create some initial depth, add more paint on the raised parts and less on the edges where shadows naturally occur. If your primer isn't black, then you can also add some black paint on the shadow parts. Leave the brown paint to dry for 2 to 4 hours.

11. For the main color, I used a metallic purple acrylic paint (Sangria Purple from Cospaint). Dab it on with a brush to get a nice layer of paint. Leave the edging and details unpainted for now, and stay away from the corners so the shadow color still shows through. Acrylic metallic paint usually dries quickly, so leave it to dry for 1 hour.

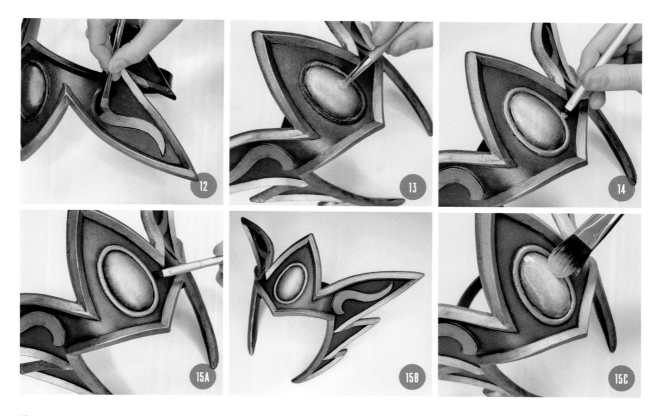

12. Apply gold metallic acrylic paint on the beveled edges and on the swirly details. (I used 14kg Gold from Cospaint.) Only paint the raised surfaces, and not the shadows, to give it even more depth.

13. To make the gem stand out, dab some pearlescent paint on it. (I used Pearl White from Cospaint.) Just use a little bit of paint on the brush, and add more layers to make it pop even more. Leave this paint to dry for 1 hour.

14. Apply silver acrylic paint on the gemstone setting. (I used Dark Silver from HexFlex.) Use a thin brush so you can be as precise as possible. Leave this to dry for 1 hour.

15. Optional: Take your paint job to the next level by creating even more shadows with black oil paint (page 32). Then, if you want, finish off by protecting your project with a layer of varnish (page 32). For this project, I recommend coating the whole piece with satin acrylic varnish and applying glossy acrylic varnish on the gem.

Get Creative! Ideas for Variations

If you don't like the spiked shape, make it round. What about a metallic blue headpiece for a Sorceress who controls the power of water? Or perhaps green, to make it more elvish looking.

This piece looks brand new, but you can add battle damage like scratches and dents to add more character to the piece with one or more of the simple techniques on page 24.

Changing the shape of the gem or adding more gems can have an interesting effect. You could also use store-bought acrylic cabochons to make the gems. They come in various colors, shapes and sizes and are translucent.

I left the strap on the back brown, because that matches my hair color. But you can paint the strap gold or the color of your own hair or wig.

MATERIALS

Combat Helmet templates (pattern sheets I and III)

1 (14 x 26-inch [35 x 66-cm]) sheet of 6mm EVA foam

1 (6 x 8-inch [15 x 20-cm]) piece of 2mm EVA foam

Contact cement

Filler (optional)

Flexible primer (black)

Acrylic paint (metallic silver)

Black oil paint (optional)

Satin (spray) varnish (optional)

TOOLS

Measuring tape

Paint marker

Craft knife

Cutting mat

Heat gun

Safety tools, including a respirator, dust mask and safety glasses (review page 16)

Rotary tool with sanding drum (120-grit), or regular sandpaper

Brushes and sponges for painting

COMBAT HELMET
With Nose Guard

This helmet is a beginner-friendly project that will fit with many costumes. The scratches and dents are made by intentionally damaging the piece with a rotary tool. To create extra depth and make the helmet more interesting, we'll be adding some strips of foam as layers on top of the helmet, and we'll also create faux rivets from thinner foam. Painting the helmet silver with a sponge instead of a brush will prevent visible brushstrokes and adds to the effect of it looking like an old piece of armor.

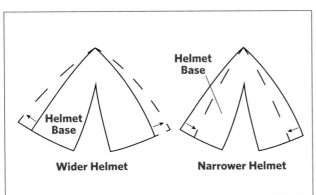

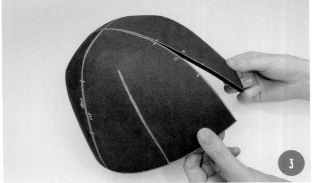

PREPARATION

Before cutting into the foam, measure around your head to see if you'll need to resize the template. Be sure to measure around the widest part of your head, at eyebrow height.

If your head is approximately 23 inches (58 cm) wide, this helmet will fit you perfectly. If your head is slightly smaller, the helmet would fit if you wear a wig underneath, or you can make the sides of the helmet base pattern piece a bit smaller.

If your head is smaller, divide the smaller amount by eight and take that amount away from each side of the helmet base pattern piece.

If your head is larger, divide the amount that it's larger by eight and add that to each side of the helmet base pattern piece.

Once you've made any necessary adjustments to your template, trace and cut the helmet base four times out of 6mm EVA foam. Also cut the 1-inch (2.5-cm)-wide bands and the nose guard piece out of 6mm EVA foam. Because

we want the nose guard to be a bit thicker than the bands, cut an additional nose guard piece out of 2mm EVA foam. Lastly, cut 22 circles with ½-inch (1.3-cm) diameters out of 2mm EVA foam.

Note: To skip the nose guard layering, you can also cut it once out of 8mm or 10mm EVA foam.

BUILDING THE HELMET BASE

1. Close the darts on all four of the helmet base pieces with the contact cement to give the helmet a rounded shape on the top so it fits your head.

2. Glue two of the helmet base pieces together to form a half helmet. Make sure to align any registration marks you copied over. Repeat this for the other two pieces to end up with two half helmets.

3. Glue the two halves together to complete the helmet base shape.

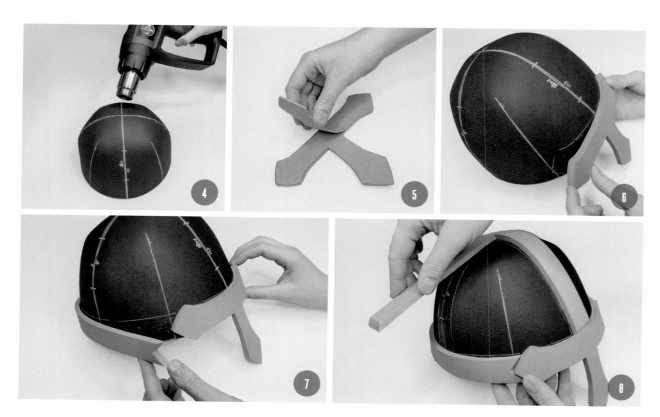

4. Heat the helmet with the heat gun. When the foam is hot, press the helmet slightly in on both sides to give it more of an oval shape so that it will fit better on your head. Be careful that it's not too hot so it's safe to touch. Hold the helmet for a few minutes in this oval shape until it's cooled down, so the foam will stay in this shape. If you want to keep it simple and don't want to add details, continue with step 10 now.

Note: After you heat-shape the helmet into an oval and let it cool down, put it on your head and feel how it fits. If it's still too large, you can cut away some material by cutting new darts into the foam and then gluing them shut. This can be a bit tricky, but it will help if you made the helmet too big.

MAKING THE NOSE GUARD

5. Take the two nose guard pieces and glue the 2mm piece on top of the 6mm piece to get a thicker nose guard. If you don't want this piece to be thicker than the decorative bands, skip this step.

6. Glue the now 8mm-thick nose guard to the front of the helmet. The bottom part of the nose guard should be left unglued. This is the part that will be in front of your nose when wearing the helmet.

ADDING DECORATIVE BANDS AND RIVETS

7. Check if the length of the decorative band is right by holding it against the helmet where it should be placed and mark the location with a paint marker. If it's too long, shorten it. Now glue the decorative band around the helmet, right at the bottom.

8. Check if the lengths of the top bands are correct by holding them against the helmet where they should be placed. One should be placed above the nose guard and reach over the top of the helmet to the back. The other two should be placed on the sides. If the bands are too long, shorten them. Also mark the places where the bands need to go on the helmet with a paint marker. Now glue the longer decorative band on the helmet, and then glue the two shorter decorative bands on the sides.

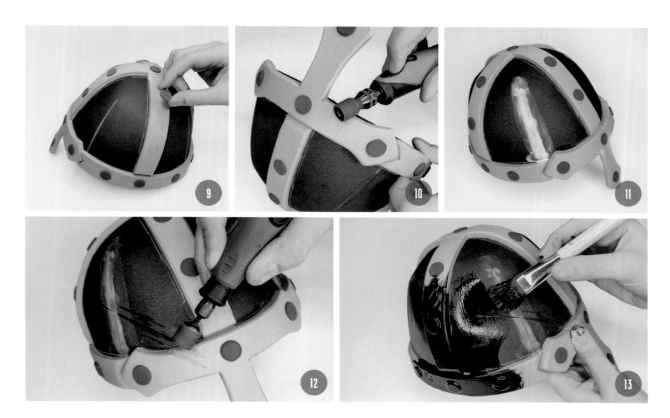

9. Decide where you want to place the 2mm faux rivets on the decorative bands and the nose guard and mark those spots with a paint marker. I put four rivets on the nose guard, nine on the band around the helmet base and nine on the bands that go across the helmet. Glue the circles on the helmet.

CLEANING UP THE EDGES

10. Using the rotary tool with 120-grit sanding drum, sand the edges of the helmet, the decorative bands and rivets to make the edges softer. Lastly, sand gently over the darts that you glued to make the seams less visible. The result of the sanding will look nicest when using a rotary tool, but you can also use regular sandpaper for this job. After the sanding is done, clean the foam piece by removing all of the dust.

OPTIONAL: SMOOTHING SEAMS WITH FILLER

11. Skip this step if the seams are already smooth from the sanding. For smoothing the seams, apply some filler

(page 23) on the seams and smooth it out after adding some water to it. Leave the filler to dry overnight, and add more layers if necessary.

CREATING BATTLE DAMAGE

12. If you want to add battle damage, review the technique on page 24.

PRIMING AND PAINTING

13. Prepare the piece for priming and painting by heat-sealing with hot air from the heat gun. When the foam is cooled down again, apply a flexible primer. Cover the complete outside of the piece, the nose guard and the inside, because that can be visible while wearing the helmet. Use as many coats of primer as needed until you like how the surface looks. I used two layers of HexFlex black. Leave the primer to dry for 2 to 4 hours.

Get Creative! Ideas for Variations

This design doesn't have too many details, but there are plenty of ways to personalize it! For example, change the paint color. Try gold or copper instead of silver.

While the nose guard is a signature part of this helmet, you can leave it off to create something simpler. Or you can extend the nose guard so it frames the eyes too.

You can wear the helmet just over your head or wear it over a chainmail cowl to get extra medieval flair.

Create more textures on this helmet by burning some designs in it with a woodburning tool or cut out beautiful designs like Celtic knots and glue them to the helmet to make it look extra fancy. Or replace the faux rivets with spikes to make the helmet look fiercer. Glue some EVA foam horns or wings to the sides of the helmet to make this piece even more unique.

14. Apply metallic silver acrylic paint on the helmet. (I used Dark Silver from HexFlex.) Dab it on with a sponge to prevent brushstrokes. Put only a little bit of paint on the sponge each time and try to stay away from the corners and any battle damage dents so the black shadow shows through, creating more depth. If you managed to keep the shadows dark and get a nice gradient in this step already, then you can skip adding oil paint in step 15. Acrylic metallic paint usually dries really quickly, so leave it to dry for 1 hour.

15. Optional: Take your paint job to the next level by creating even more shadows with black oil paint (page 32). In the project shown here, I skipped this step because the shadows were already looking good. Finish off by protecting your project with a layer of varnish (page 32). For this project, I recommend coating the whole piece with satin acrylic varnish.

MATERIALS

Curved Horns templates (pattern sheets I and II)

1 (12 x 24–inch [30 x 60–cm]) sheet of 4mm EVA foam

4 (1 x 2-inch [2.5 x 5-cm]) pieces of 2mm EVA foam

Contact cement

Foam clay

20 inches (50 cm) of metal wire (I used 1mm-thick metal wire)

1 plastic headband

Painter's tape

Flexible primer (black)

Acrylic paint (dark brown and beige)

Matte (spray) varnish (optional)

TOOLS

Paint marker

Pliers, for cutting and bending metal wire

Craft knife

Cutting mat

Wooden clay modeling tool

Safety tools, including a respirator (review page 16)

Brushes and sponges for painting

CURVED HORNS
With Foam Clay Texture

With this project, we're going to use foam clay to create horns with an interesting organic texture. The soft foam clay allows for lots of freedom to create different textures. These horns have a nice curve to them so they will look good from every angle. And they are hollow, which makes them super lightweight and comfortable to wear (even with the foam clay texturing on them). We'll be adding these horns to a headband, and because we aren't gluing them down, you'll be able to adjust the placement of the horns on your head even after the project is finished. Being so universal, these horns can fit with many different costumes, ranging from a graceful faun-style wood elf to a fierce barbarian warrior.

PREPARATION

With this project, we're using a headband to mount the horns. Make sure you pick one that fits you well and try to find one with "teeth" so that it stays on better.

With the pliers, cut the metal wire into four equally sized pieces.

Use your templates to trace and cut pieces A, B and C for the horns out of 4mm EVA foam. Do the same mirrored for the other horn, so you'll end up with six pieces of foam. When cutting the foam, make sure to follow the template and cut the tips of the horns at an inward angle. This will make gluing the tips together nice and tight much easier. See page 17 for a more detailed explanation about cutting foam.

Cut four (2 x 1-inch [5 x 2.5-cm]) strips of 2mm EVA foam. These will be used to secure the ends of the metal wire to the inside of the horns so you can attach them to the headband.

You'll need quite a lot of foam clay to cover these horns, so make sure your pot of foam clay is still relatively full when you start this project.

BUILDING THE HORNS

1. Take pieces B and C for one horn and apply a thin layer of contact cement to both edges marked with the > shaped registration marks. Once the glue is tacky, attach the two pieces, making sure to match up any > shaped registration marks. Sometimes it may feel like the registration marks are off, but with a little force you should be able to make them fit. This will ensure the horns get their curved shape in the end.

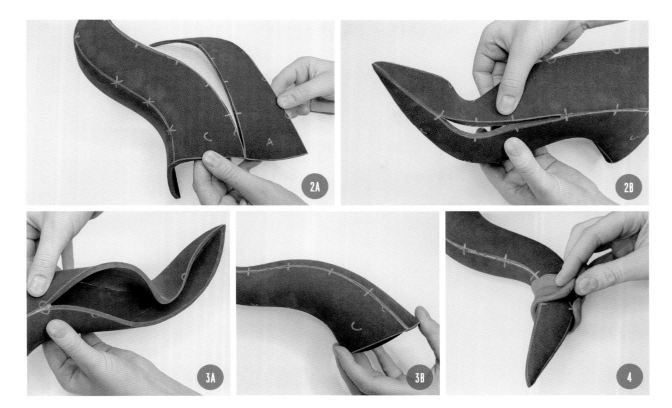

2. Take piece A for the same horn and apply a thin layer of contact cement to both edges marked with the — shaped registration marks. Once the glue is tacky, attach the two pieces, making sure to match up any — shaped registration marks. Here again, it's possible that you will need to force the foam a bit to make the registration marks align.

3. Apply contact cement to the two remaining edges of piece A and B, marked with the half-circle shaped registration marks. Attach them, making sure the half-circles align, so the horn is completely closed (only the bottom is still open). Now you can see the beautiful final curved shape of the horn! Repeat steps 1, 2 and 3 for the other horn.

Note: If you like how the horns look at this point and don't want to use foam clay, or don't have any foam clay, then continue with step 8 now.

TEXTURING WITH FOAM CLAY

4. We're going to be creating multiple layers of foam clay, so feel free to sketch some lines on the horn if you need some guidance.

Apply a bit of water on the horn where you want to add the first layer of texture. Take some foam clay out of the pot, flatten it and fold it around the horn. Notice that we're not applying foam clay on the very tip of the horn just yet. This is because it's convenient if you can hold the tip of the horn while working on the foam clay layers. So, leave this tip free of foam clay until later.

Note: Remember to close the pot of foam clay each time you take something out to prevent it from drying out.

5. Smooth out the foam clay at the bottom of the layer, and leave it bulkier at the top. With a wooden clay modeling tool, carve some lines in the soft foam clay to make it look like realistic horn texture. If you have time, leave the foam clay to air-dry overnight. Otherwise continue directly with the next steps, being careful not to not touch the previous layer of soft foam clay when you work on the next.

6. Apply a bit of water on the horn, right below where you added the foam clay. Then take some extra foam clay out of the pot (a bit more this time, because this part of the horn will be thicker and need more clay to cover it). Now flatten the foam clay and fold it around the horn, just covering the previous foam clay layer.

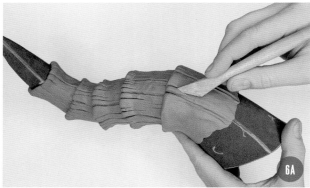

Smooth out the bottom of this layer and leave the top bulky. Carve lines in the foam clay using a clay modeling tool to create texture. Repeat this step as many times as you need until you reach the base of the horn. I added six layers of foam clay to my horn.

Then repeat the same steps for the other horn, so you end up with two horns that are covered in foam clay layers. Just the tips of the horns won't be covered with foam clay yet. Now leave the foam clay on the horns to dry overnight.

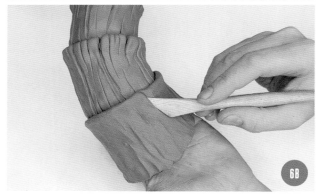

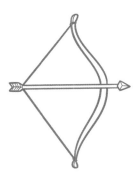

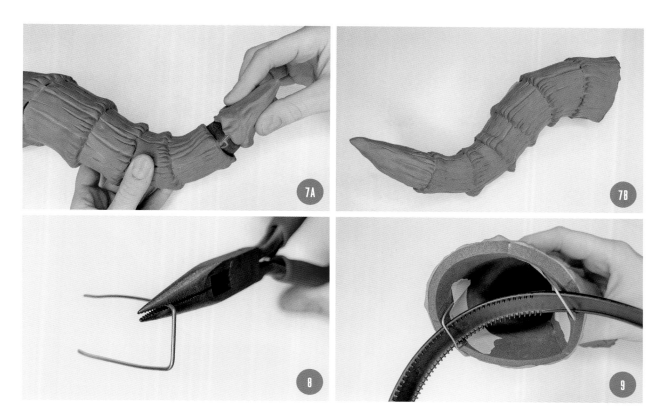

7. After the foam clay on the horns has air-dried overnight, it won't be completely cured, but for this step that is OK. It will be cured enough to touch it and to hold it without deforming it.

Take one horn and apply a bit of water on the tip. Then take some foam clay out of the pot and cover the tip of the horn with it. Add some texture to the soft foam clay by carving lines in it with the wooden modeling tool. Repeat this for the other horn. Now set the horns aside to let the foam clay air-dry for at least 48 hours.

MAKE THEM WEARABLE

8. For each horn, take two of the four metal wire pieces and bend two corners in them, using the pair of pliers. Check the width of the headband to make sure it will fit snug through the wire.

9. Put both bent metal wire pieces inside the base of the horn, leaving them sticking out a bit so they will fit over the headband. Tape them on temporarily. Repeat this for the other horn, and then put the headband through these four metal loops. Now the horns are temporarily attached to the headband, and you can try it on your head to see if you like the placement and direction of the horns. Change the direction of the horns by removing the tape, adjusting the location of the metal wires and putting the tape back on again. Repeat this until you like the placement of the horns. Now take the tape away and mark the foam with a paint marker where the metal wires need to sit.

Note: How high the horns sit on your head doesn't really matter since you will still be able to move them higher and lower when you are finished with this project.

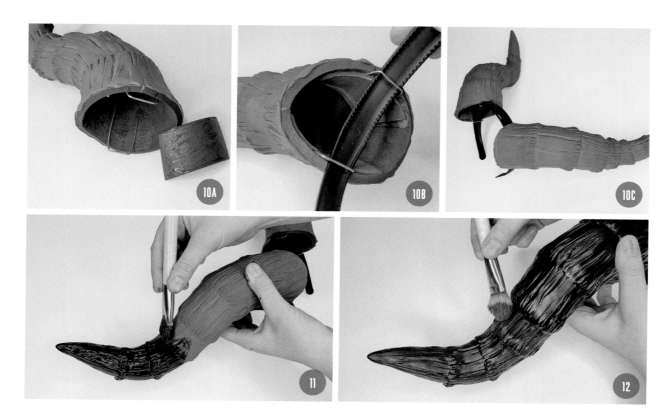

10. For each horn, take 2 pieces of the 1 x 2-inch (2.5 x 5-cm) 2mm EVA foam and apply a thin layer of contact cement to both the thin piece of foam and to the inside of the horn where you want to secure the metal wire. Put the metal wire on the still wet glue and it should keep it in place. Once the glue is tacky, press the rectangle of foam on top of the metal wire to secure it tightly. Now you can slide the horns over the headband through the two metal loops. Make sure not to break the plastic teeth on the headband. These are important to keep the horns at the height where you want to wear them. Because of this trick, the horns don't need to be glued to the headband. If you want to glue the horns on the headband, you can do that now by adding some extra glue. This is optional.

The horns are now wearable!

PRIMING AND PAINTING

11. Apply a flexible primer to the entire outside of each horn. Use as many coats of primer as needed until you like how the surface looks. With foam clay you'll find it's already super smooth, so you'll need fewer layers of primer than for regular EVA foam. I used one layer of HexFlex black. Leave the primer to dry for 2 to 4 hours.

12. Decide which color the horns are going to be and start with the darkest version of this color. I chose brown, so I used dark brown acrylic paint for this first layer of color. Apply the dark brown acrylic paint by dry brushing. Leave the carved-in texture lines black by only painting the raised parts to give some depth because the black will look like shadows. To do this, don't take too much paint on your brush, and paint in the opposite direction of the lines. Leave the paint to dry for 2 to 4 hours.

13. Mix a lighter shade of your color (by combining your color and beige or white) and with a sponge, paint on the upper halves of each foam clay layer. Only put a little bit of paint on the sponge each time and don't press down on the horns too hard, so you will only get paint on the raised parts and not inside the carved lines. Try to form a gradient on the layers, where the top of each layer is lighter than the bottom. Build up these highlights by going over it again with lighter shades of your color, and ending with the pure beige color on just the top edges of the foam clay layers. This will create a lot of depth to your horns. Between each layer of paint, wait until the last layer has dried, which usually takes 1 to 2 hours for dry brushing.

14. Leave the paint job to fully dry overnight and then optionally add a layer of matte varnish to protect it. Either spray or paint over the paint with a matte acrylic varnish (page 32). For this project I used a brush-on matte acrylic varnish and applied one layer.

Get Creative! Ideas for Variations

Did you craft the Enchanted Elven Ears on page 54? Combine the horns with the elf ears on the same headband!

If you don't like working with foam clay, or can't find it, there are other ways to create texture on the horns. Try using a rotary tool with a sanding drum attached to it to carve texture lines into the horns or a woodburning tool to burn texture lines into the foam, similar to the Deadly Horned Pauldrons (page 59). If the horns are too long, cut off a part at the base before adding the foam clay.

Try different colors, like red. Even pearlescent colors would make great fairy-like horns! Make the horns extra fancy by adding some jewelry on them like piercings or bands made with EVA foam and then paint them gold or silver.

MATERIALS

Enchanted Elven Ears templates (digital pattern)

1 (8 x 6-inch [20 x 15-cm]) sheet of 4mm EVA foam

1 (8 x 8-inch [20 x 20-cm]) piece of 2mm EVA foam

Contact cement

1 plastic headband

Flexible primer (black)

Acrylic paint (dark brown and beige)

Matte (spray) varnish (optional)

TOOLS

Paint marker

Craft knife

Cutting mat

Heat gun

Safety tools, including a respirator, dust mask and safety glasses (review page 16)

Rotary tool with sanding drum (120-grit), or regular sandpaper

Brushes and sponges for painting

ENCHANTED ELVEN EARS

With EVA foam, you can create some elegant elven ears for your costumes. This project is really simple and can be worn over your hair or a wig. To make it look like they're really your ears, let some locks of your hair hang loose, framing your face on both sides. That way the hair will hide the headband and the base of the ears, making them look more realistic.

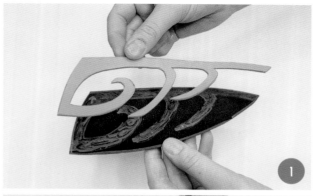

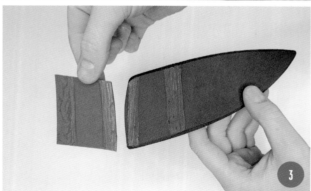

PREPARATION

Use your template to trace and cut the ear base out of 4mm EVA foam twice (once mirrored). Using the thinner 2mm EVA foam, cut out the detail layer and the backing piece both twice (once mirrored).

In this project, we're going to use a headband to make these ears wearable so make sure you choose one that fits you well.

ASSEMBLING THE EARS

1. Put the 2mm-thick detail layer on the 4mm-thick ear base and with a paint marker, trace around it. Then apply a thin layer of contact cement on both the detail layer and on the part that you just marked with a paint marker. When the glue is tacky, press the detail layer firmly onto the ear base. Repeat this for the other ear and make sure it's mirrored.

Optional: Heat the ears with the heat gun. When the foam is hot, you can bend the tips outwards to give the ears some dimension (for more on heat shaping, see page 24).

2. Using the rotary tool with 120-grit sanding drum, sand the edges of the ears smooth. Also sand the edges of the detail layer to make the edges softer and less harsh. This works best when using a rotary tool, but you can also use regular sandpaper. After the sanding is done, clean the foam piece by removing all of the dust.

MAKE THEM WEARABLE

3. Turn the ear upside down so the back is now visible. Lay the headband on the back of the ear and draw a line on either side to indicate where the headband will sit. Then take one of the backing pieces and apply a thin layer of contact cement to both the backing layer and the back of the ear, leaving the strip for the headband free of glue. This will allow the ears to be removed from the headband.

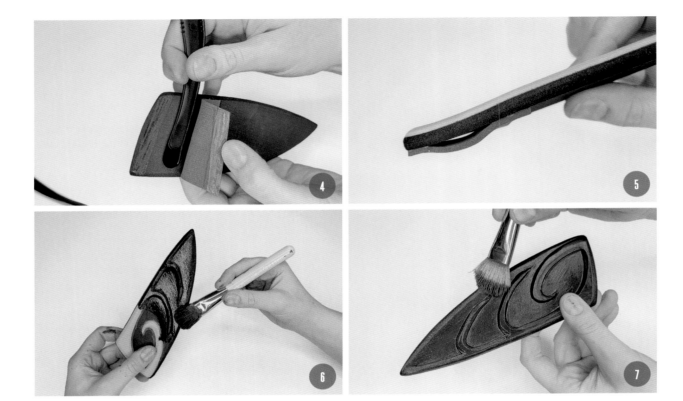

4. When the glue is tacky, put the headband on the back of the ear, right in the middle where there is no glue, and then press the backing piece on the back of the ear so it covers the headband.

5. Take the headband out of the ear and you'll notice that the backing piece is a bit open, leaving room for the headband. Now the ear can be put on the headband, and it can also be taken off again. If you want a more permanent solution, you can choose to glue the ears directly to the headband.

PRIMING AND PAINTING

6. Prepare the piece for priming and painting by heat-sealing it by blowing hot air over the foam with the heat gun. When the foam is cooled down again, apply a flexible primer to the ear and cover the complete front and back. Use as many coats of primer as needed until you like how the surface looks. I used two layers of HexFlex black. Leave the primer to dry for 2 to 4 hours.

7. Decide which color the ears are going to be and start with the darkest version of this color. I chose to paint these in a color that matches my foundation makeup which is a rather pale tone. Skin tones can be difficult to achieve with paint, but I chose to start with dark brown for the shadow layer. Apply the darkest paint on the complete front and back of the ear. Leave the paint to dry for 2 to 4 hours.

8. Mix a lighter shade of brown (by combining dark brown and beige or white) and with a sponge, dab this color on the ear. Only put a little bit of paint on the sponge each time and don't press down on the ears too hard, so you only get paint on the raised detail parts and not inside the shadow lines. Build up these highlights by going over it again with lighter shades of brown, and end with the pure beige color. This will create a feeling of depth. Between each layer of paint, wait until the last layer has dried, which usually takes 1 to 2 hours when you add such light layers of paint each time.

9. Leave the paint job to fully dry overnight and then optionally add a layer of varnish to protect it (page 32). I used brush-on matte acrylic varnish and applied one layer.

To wear the ears, slide them on both ends of the headband. While wearing the headband, adjust the ears higher or lower until you like the position of them.

Get Creative! Ideas for Variations

Did you also craft the Curved Horns on page 47? Combine the elf ears with the horns on the same headband!

Of course, these ears can be worn on a headband like in the example, but you can also choose to glue them right onto a costume like on a hooded cape, for example. That way you can simply put the hood on your head and the ears will be in place.

If the ears from this project are too big for your costume or perhaps too small, simply adjust the template to change the size of the ears. You can also change the shape to resemble various fantasy creatures. These ears are styled like super-long elf ears, but why not make cool ears for a goblin, imp or even a mermaid? Use your imagination to come up with new ear designs to craft.

You can paint these ears in your own natural skin tone or create fantasy colors like green for a dragon character or teal for a mermaid. To give the ears more style, add some jewelry, such as earrings or studs.

SHOULDER ARMOR

DEADLY HORNED PAULDRONS

With Wood Grain Texture

With this shoulder armor piece, we're going to create some awesome wood grain texture in the foam—very fitting for a wood elf character. This technique may be a bit tricky at first, but before you know it, you'll want to burn a wood texture into every foam project! This technique also works on other armor pieces or even props like "wooden" shields or tankards. For the horns, we'll use a thinner foam, which will make it easier to glue the tips as neatly as possible. You can make one pauldron for your costume and wear it over one shoulder, or make one for each shoulder. The materials listed are for two pauldrons.

MATERIALS

Deadly Horned Pauldrons templates (digital pattern)

1 (2 x 2-ft [60 x 60-cm]) sheet of 6mm EVA foam

1 (14 x 12-inch [35 x 30-cm]) piece of 4mm EVA foam

1 (4 x 2-inch [10 x 5-cm]) piece of 2mm EVA foam

6 thin strips of stretchy jersey fabric (moss green)

Contact cement

4 metal D-rings (I used 1-inch [2.5-cm]-wide D-rings)

Flexible primer (black)

Acrylic paint (dark brown, light brown and beige)

Matte (spray) varnish (optional)

TOOLS

Paint marker

Craft knife

Cutting mat

Measuring tape

Heat gun

Soldering iron or wood-burning tool

Safety tools, including a respirator, dust mask and safety glasses (review page 16)

Brushes for painting

Needle and thread (for the braided straps)

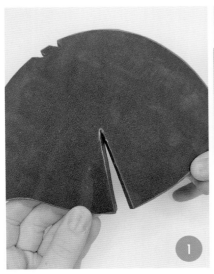
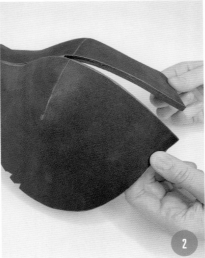

PREPARATION

To make both pauldrons, use your template to trace and cut the pauldron base out of the 6mm EVA foam four times (twice mirrored). Cut out both horn shapes four times (twice mirrored for each horn) from the thinner 4mm EVA foam. For the horns, it's important to cut the foam at an inward angle at the tips. This will make it easier to glue the tips together nice and tight. On the template, it's marked where to make the angled cut. See pages 17 to 19 for a more detailed explanation about cutting foam.

Cut four (2 x 1–inch [5 x 2.5–cm]) strips of 2mm EVA foam. These will be used to attach some D-rings to the pauldrons.

Now take some measurements for the jersey fabric straps that will be used to attach the armor to your body. Measure from the front of your shoulder, going under the opposite armpit, over the back and to the back of the shoulder. For me, this was about 28 inches (70 cm). The straps will need to be tied on the D-rings, so the straps will need to be up to 1 foot (30 cm) longer than the measurement you took. So, I needed straps that were 3 feet (90 cm) long. If you want to make the straps from elastic material and braid it to look nice, like I did, then cut six (1-inch [2.5-cm]-wide) strips that are each 3 feet (90 cm) long. You will need three for each pauldron, so six in total for both pauldrons. If you want to use rope or yarn, simply use that instead. Just keep in mind that those won't be elastic so it could be a bit less comfortable to wear.

BUILDING THE PAULDRON BASE

1. Close the darts on both of the pauldron base pieces using the contact cement. This dart will help to give the pauldron a rounded shape on the top so it fits nicely on the shoulders.

2. Glue both halves of the pauldron together along the top edge. You can use the closed dart as a registration mark for gluing to make the armor piece as symmetrical as possible.

3. After the glue has fully set, heat the armor piece with the heat gun. When the foam is hot, you can shape it to be more rounded and to curl up at the edges. Hold the armor piece for a few minutes in the desired shape until it's cooled down, so the foam will stay in this shape. Repeat steps 1 through 3 for the second pauldron.

Note: To make this project even more beginner friendly, feel free to skip the horns and texturing. Just create the base shape and paint the armor pieces. They will still look awesome! And when you feel more advanced, you can follow all the steps to create the wood grain texture and horns.

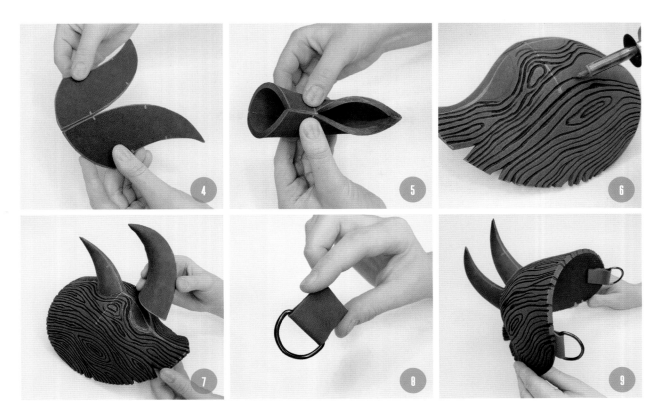

ASSEMBLING THE HORNS

4. Apply contact cement to the back edges of the mirrored horn pieces. When the glue is tacky, connect the two foam pieces.

5. Once that side is attached, apply contact cement to the two remaining edges and attach them so the horn is completely closed (except the bottom). Repeat these steps for the other horns. Once all four horns are finished (two small and two larger), you can mark the spots on the pauldrons where you want to place the horns by tracing them with a paint marker.

CREATING WOOD GRAIN TEXTURE

6. Sketch some wood grain on the pauldrons as a guide for making the texture. Don't just make straight lines, but also add some circles and gnarly lines, since this will give more character to the final piece.

Turn on your soldering iron or woodburning tool, and when it's heated up, start burning lines into the foam to create the wood grain texture. Press harder to create deeper, thicker lines or gentler for narrower, thinner lines.

7. Glue the horns on the pauldrons. Heat the pauldrons with the heat gun to seal them and close the pores of the foam to prepare it for painting.

ADDING D-RINGS TO THE PAULDRONS

8. Apply contact cement on both ends of one of the 2mm EVA strips. When the glue is almost dry, fold the foam strip through the D-ring and press it closed so the metal ring is attached. Repeat this step for the rest of the D-rings.

9. Glue the piece of foam with the D-ring to the inside of the pauldrons. Do this on the front and on the back, so you can add a string or straps for wearing the armor pieces.

PRIMING AND PAINTING

10. Apply a black flexible primer onto the armor pieces. Also apply some primer on the underside at the edges, where the raw foam color could still show while wearing the armor. Use as many coats of primer as needed until you like how the surface looks. I used two layers of HexFlex black. If your primer isn't black, you can either mix some black acrylic paint into the primer before applying it or paint the pauldrons black with some acrylic paint after the primer is dry, which usually takes 2 to 4 hours.

11. When the black base layer is dry, apply a layer of brown acrylic paint to the armor pieces. Make sure to leave the texture lines black by only painting on the raised parts. This already gives some depth because the black will look like a shadow. To do this, don't take too much paint on your brush, and paint in the opposite direction of the lines. Also apply some brown lines on the horns to give them more dimension.

After the dry brushing, take a smaller brush and refine some of the parts that didn't get enough paint coverage. Now leave the paint to dry for 2 to 4 hours before moving on to the next step.

12. Mix a lighter color of brown (with dark brown and either beige or white) and with a thin brush, paint some lines to create highlights (page 31). Just randomly select lines that you want to highlight. Also highlight the circles in the wood grain so that they stand out more. You can build up the highlights by going over them again with the pure beige color to make some of the lines pop even more.

13. Leave the paint job to fully dry overnight, and then optionally add a layer of matte varnish to protect it (page 32).

Get Creative! Ideas for Variations

If you don't like the look of the horns on the pauldrons, you can use different shaped horns or simply leave them off. Decorate your pauldrons even more by sculpting mushrooms and autumn leaves out of foam clay. Add them on the pauldrons with a little bit of water while the clay shapes are still soft, or glue them on the pauldrons after the clay shapes have fully air-dried.

In this example, I used stretchy fabric, which I braided for the armor attachment. But it's also possible to sew a belt with a buckle and use that for wearing the armor piece. Or to make it even easier, you could simply tie some rope or yarn to the armor piece and use that.

For these pauldrons, I used a matte acrylic varnish to protect the paint job. A glossy varnish wouldn't look good on the wood texture. But if you want the horns to be extra shiny, you can apply a glossy varnish on just the horns. This will add even more texture to the final product.

MAKE THEM WEARABLE

14. For each pauldron, take three long strips of jersey fabric and braid them.

Close the two ends of the braid with some hand stitches using the needle and thread so they won't come undone.

15. Tie the strap to the D-rings. Then you can wear your finished armor piece by simply putting it on your shoulder, and then placing the stretchy strap under your arm on the other side. Repeat this for the other pauldron and wear the straps crossed over your chest.

MATERIALS

Noble Layered Pauldrons templates (pattern sheets IV and V)

1 (14 x 24-inch [35 x 60-cm]) sheet of 6mm EVA foam

1 (10 x 10-inch [25 x 25-cm]) piece of 2mm EVA foam

Contact cement

63 inches (160 cm) of EVA foam prefab triangular bevel (I used 10mm wide, high profile)

55 inches (140 cm) of EVA foam prefab triangular bevel (I used 10mm wide, low profile)

12 inches (30 cm) of EVA foam prefab half-round dowel (I used 5mm wide)

Foam clay

Filler (optional)

4 metal D-rings (I used 1-inch [2.5-cm]-wide D-rings)

Elastic (purple)

1 (1½-inch [4-cm]) piece of ¾-inch (2-cm)-wide Velcro

2 (¾-inch [2-cm]-wide) strips of jersey fabric (purple)

Flexible primer (black)

Acrylic paint (dark brown, metallic purple, pearl, gold and silver)

Oil paint (black) (optional)

Satin and glossy (spray) varnish (optional)

NOBLE LAYERED PAULDRONS
With Elegant Swirls

These pointy pauldrons are elegantly curved, and each one consists of two layers to make the silhouette extra interesting. The bottom layer also helps keep the top layer upright, so it's not just pretty, but functional too. In this project, we'll be using prefab EVA foam bevels to create beautiful edges on the armor piece. If you are short on time because the convention is coming up fast, you'll be so thankful that these premade foam shapes exist!

To decorate the pauldrons, we're using some 2mm EVA foam to create swirly designs, which we will glue on the pauldrons as an extra detail layer. With foam clay, we'll sculpt pretty faux gems to give the armor extra style. When you make the Magical Sorceress' Breastplate (page 105), you can attach these pauldrons to the front of the breastplate to make them stay on your shoulders. Without the breastplate, you can use a fabric strap around your chest to make the shoulder armor pieces stay on.

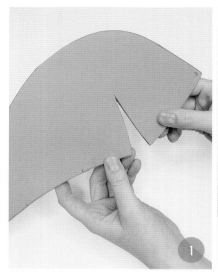
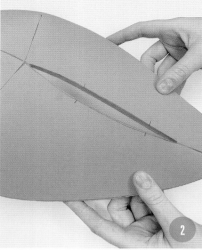

TOOLS

Paint marker

Craft knife

Cutting mat

Heat gun

Safety tools, including a respirator, dust mask and safety glasses (review page 16)

Rotary tool with sanding drum (120-grit) or regular sandpaper

Wooden clay modeling tool (optional)

Brushes for painting

Sewing machine or needle and thread

Pin or a clip

Measuring tape

PREPARATION

Use your template to trace and cut the pauldron base upper layer out of the 6mm EVA foam four times (twice mirrored). Cut the pauldron base's lower layer out of 6mm EVA foam four times (twice mirrored).

Cut out the swirly details four times (twice mirrored) from the thin 2mm EVA foam.

Cut four (2 x 1–inch [5 x 2.5–cm]) strips of 2mm EVA foam. These will be used to attach D-rings to the pauldrons.

BUILDING THE BASE PIECES

1. Close the darts on both pauldron base pieces for the upper layer, using the contact cement. This dart will help give the pauldron a rounded shape on the top so it fits nicely on the shoulders.

2. Glue both halves of the pauldron *upper* layer together along the edge. Use the registration marks you copied over as a guide for connecting the pieces.

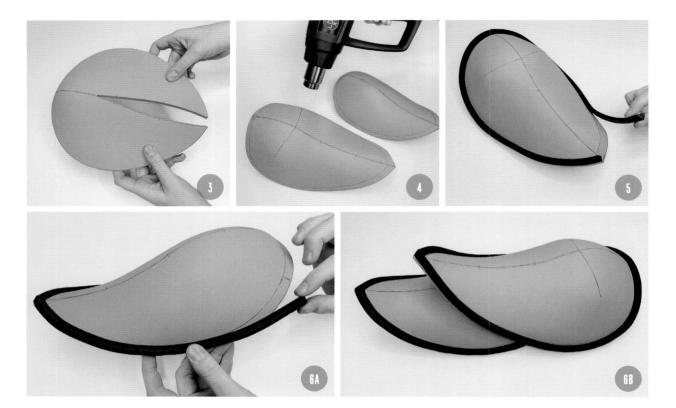

3. Glue both halves of the pauldron bottom layer together along the edge, using the registration marks as a guide for connecting the pieces. Repeat steps 1, 2 and 3 for both pauldrons.

4. After the glue has fully set on all four pauldron pieces, heat them with the heat gun. When the foam is hot, shape it to be more rounded and to curl up at the edges a little bit. Hold the armor piece for a few minutes in the desired shape until it's cooled down, so the foam will stay in this shape. Repeat these steps for all four pauldron parts. If you want to keep it simple and don't want to add details, you can skip steps 5 through 9.

DECORATING THE EDGES AND ADDING DETAILS

5. Measure, cut and glue the triangular-shaped *high-profile* bevel along the edges of the pauldron upper layer base. To achieve nice pointy corners, make sure to cut the ends diagonally. Remember to also glue the ends where any bevels meet. Repeat for the other pauldron.

Note: Each piece of bevel will vary in length, so to avoid mixing them up, write numbers or letters on them and also on the corresponding part of the armor pieces where they need to go.

6. Measure, cut and glue the triangular-shaped *low-profile* bevel along the edges of the pauldron bottom layer base. Remember to cut the ends diagonally for nice pointy corners and glue the ends where any bevels meet. Repeat this for the other pauldron.

You will need two pieces of bevel for each pauldron bottom layer. The round edges of the bottom layers should stay empty, since they'll be used to attach the upper layer. On the template, it is marked where to place the bevel.

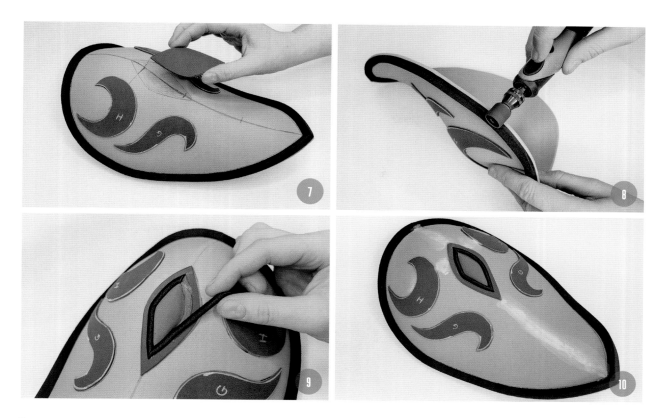

7. Take the ten swirly detail pieces, five for each pauldron, and decide where you want them to go on the upper layers. Then glue them on with contact cement as symmetrically as possible.

CLEANING UP THE EDGES

8. Using the rotary tool with 120-grit sanding drum, sand the edges of the pauldron pieces smooth. The transition between the glued-on bevels and the pauldron pieces will get super smooth in this step. Also sand the glue seams smooth. The result of the sanding will look nicest when using a rotary tool, but you can also use regular sandpaper for this job. After the sanding is done, clean the foam piece by removing all of the dust.

CREATING FAUX GEMSTONES

9. For creating the foam clay faux gemstones on the upper layer of the pauldrons, use the same technique as described in steps 6 through 7 of the Royal Headpiece (page 39). But instead of sculpting an oval shape, make it a diamond shape.

Because the gem is diamond shaped, you will need to make the gemstone settings out of two pieces of foam dowel that are both cut diagonally at the ends, instead of just one piece. This will make the gemstone setting's top and bottom more pointed to better follow the shape of the gem. Repeat these steps for both of the pauldron upper layer pieces.

OPTIONAL: SMOOTHING SEAMS WITH FILLER

10. Skip this step if the glue seams are already smooth from the sanding. For smoothing seams, apply some filler (page 23) on the seams and smooth it out after adding some water to it. Leave the filler to dry overnight, and add more layers if necessary.

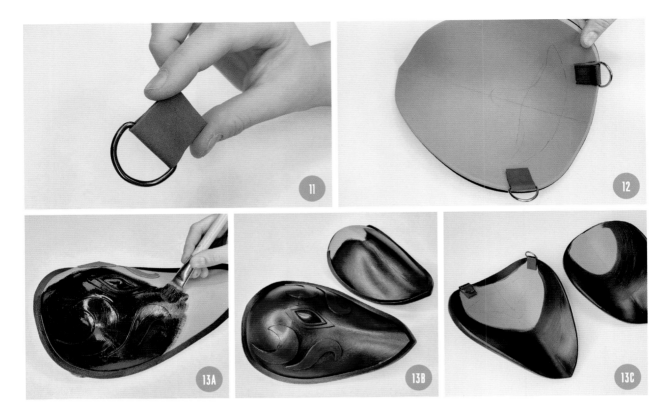

ADDING D-RINGS TO THE PAULDRONS

11. Apply some contact cement to both ends of the strips of 2mm EVA foam. When the glue is almost dry, fold the foam strip through the D-ring and press it closed so the metal ring is attached. Repeat this for the rest of the D-rings.

12. Glue the pieces of foam with the D-rings on the wider inside of the *upper* layers that sit closer to the neck, so you can add elastic and strings here later for wearing the armor pieces. On the side that will be facing the front of your body, the D-ring needs to sit lower, while on the back it needs to sit higher.

Now prepare all four foam pieces for priming and painting by heat-sealing them by blowing hot air over the foam with the heat gun. Make sure to avoid the foam clay though, because it can get damaged by the heat. Leave the piece to cool before continuing with the next step.

PRIMING AND PAINTING

13. Apply a flexible primer onto all four foam pieces. For the upper layers, cover the complete outside of the piece and also a large part of the underside, because that will show when the armor piece is worn. On the templates, it is marked where the two layers need to be glued together later. Leave those spots unprimed so the glue will adhere better later.

For the bottom layers, cover most of the outside (leaving the part where it will be glued under the upper layer free of primer) and also cover most of the underside. Just leave the part of the underside unprimed where it will rest on your shoulder. This is for comfort reasons.

Images 13B and 13C show where I left the foam free of primer. I took these after adding the brown acrylic paint in step 14, but you can still get the idea. Use as many coats of primer as needed until you like how the surface looks. I used two layers of HexFlex black. Leave the primer to dry for 2 to 4 hours.

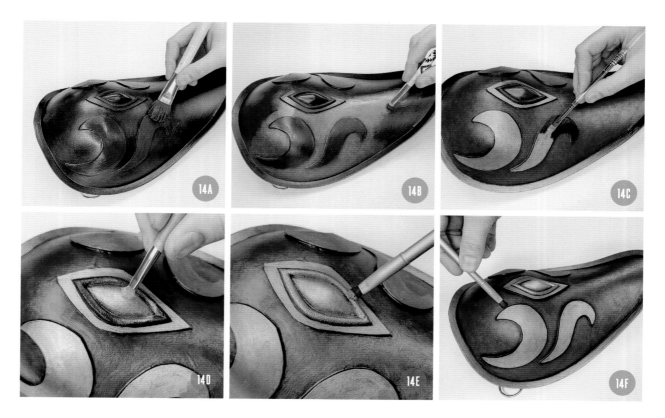

14. For painting the pauldrons, use the same technique as described in steps 10 through 14 of the Royal Headpiece (pages 40 and 41).

Optional: Then take your paint job to the next level by creating even more shadows with black oil paint (page 32).

Note: If you chose to apply oil paint shadows, when continuing with the next step, make sure to be careful to not touch the parts where you applied oil paint in order to not smudge the paint.

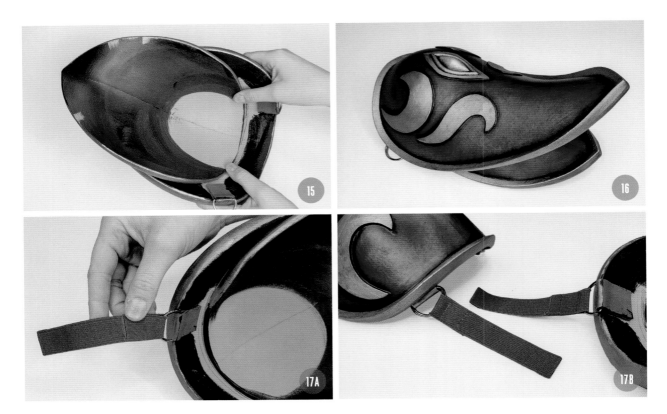

COMBINE THE TOP AND BOTTOM LAYERS

15. Apply a thin layer of contact cement on both the top of the bottom layer and underneath the upper layer of the pauldron. Those are the parts where you applied no primer or paint. When the glue is tacky, press the upper layer on top of the bottom layer to form one, layered pauldron.

Repeat this step for the other pauldron, and try to make the silhouette as symmetrical as possible.

FINISH WITH SOME VARNISH

16. Optionally, finish off the paint job by protecting your project with a layer of varnish (page 32). For this project, I recommend coating the whole piece with satin acrylic varnish, and applying glossy acrylic varnish on the gem. Leave the varnished pieces to dry overnight before continuing to the next steps.

Note: If you applied the oil paint shadows, go for the spray varnish to coat the whole piece. Oil paint dries very slowly, and it can take multiple weeks to dry, and if you apply a brush-on varnish, you could smear out the oil paint in this step.

MAKE THEM WEARABLE

17. Now that the pauldrons are crafted, use a piece of ribbon, shoelace or yarn to find out what length of elastic you will need to connect the pauldrons in the back. I used two 6-inch (15-cm)-long pieces of ¾-inch (2-cm)-wide purple elastic and some Velcro to attach the back D-rings together.

Take the end of one of the pieces of purple elastic, bring it through one of the D-rings and fold it over. Sew the folded elastic down, so it will stay connected to the D-ring. I used a sewing machine for this, but it can also be sewn by hand with a needle and thread. Repeat this for the other pauldron.

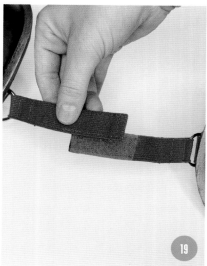

18. Overlap the two ends of the elastic and attach them temporarily by putting a pin through them or by using a clip. Now try the pauldrons on your own shoulders and decide if the elastic is the correct length. If the pauldrons fall off your shoulders, make the elastic shorter by moving the pin or clip. Once you are happy with the length, measure that both elastic pieces overlap by 2 inches (5 cm). Now cut the elastics to size.

19. Fold the last ½ inch (1.3 cm) of the elastic over and sew the Velcro on top of it. Sew the hook part on top of one elastic, and the loop part on the bottom of the other. I used a sewing machine to sew this down, but you can also sew it by hand with needle and thread.

20. Use the strips of jersey fabric to connect the front D-rings on the pauldrons with D-rings on a chestplate. Or to wear it without a chestplate, you can wear a longer strip of fabric across your chest and weave it through the front D-rings around to your back and tie the ends together. Another option is to sew some elastic with Velcro to the shoulder straps of the breastplate on the front. That option is described in the Magical Sorceress' Breastplate (page 105).

Get Creative! Ideas for Variations

If you don't like the silhouette, you can adjust the template to make the ends more rounded. Try making them shorter or longer to fit your character design needs perfectly.

Different colors will automatically give off a completely different vibe. Go for teal with silver details for example for an icy frost wizard.

With these straps, the pauldrons should stay on well, but if you want more security, you can add some straps to the bottom layers of the pauldrons that are worn over your upper arms.

EVA foam prefabs, like the triangular bevels, can be pricey if you buy a lot of them. For a more cost-effective option, learn how to make your own on page 25.

MATERIALS

Battleworn Shoulder Armor and Gorget templates (digital pattern)

1 (18 x 36–inch [45 x 90-cm]) sheet of 6mm EVA foam

1 (13½-foot [4.1-m] strip of ½-inch (1-cm)-wide 2mm EVA foam

1 (1.5 x 3-inch [4 x 8-cm]) piece of 2mm EVA foam

1 (4½-inch [12-cm]) piece of ¾-inch (2-cm)-wide Velcro

Contact cement

Filler (optional)

1 glue stick for hot glue gun

Flexible primer (black)

Acrylic paint (dark brown, silver and gold)

Oil paint (black) (optional)

Satin (spray) varnish (optional)

TOOLS

Paint marker

Craft knife

Cutting mat

Measuring tape

Heat gun

Safety tools, including a respirator, dust mask and safety glasses (review page 16)

Rotary tool with sanding drum (120-grit), or regular sandpaper

Hot glue gun

Brushes and sponges for painting

BATTLEWORN SHOULDER ARMOR AND GORGET
With Star-Shaped Rondels

With this project, we are going to use the undercut technique (page 19) on some EVA foam to create three-dimensional, star-shaped rondels to decorate this shoulder armor. These star-shaped pieces add more protection in battle and above all, they just look epic. These pauldrons are decorated with a knight's crest, and beneath that there are two extra layers to cover the upper arm. The shoulder pieces are quite bulky and will fit many people. And if you don't like sewing, that is good news for you! These pauldrons are held in place by a piece of neck armor called a gorget. That's why they won't need any other form of attachments like straps. The shoulder armor with gorget will look absolutely epic worn on top of a chestplate, like the Knight Chestplate on page 114. But a chestplate isn't mandatory. This shoulder armor also looks really cool over a simple tunic or medieval-style dress.

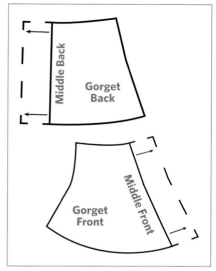

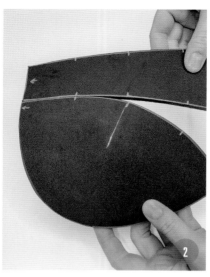

PREPARATION

Use your template to trace and cut the pauldron upper layer side pieces out of 6mm EVA foam four times (twice mirrored). Cut the pauldron upper layer center pieces out of the 6mm EVA foam twice.

Cut the pauldron base middle and bottom layers out of 6mm EVA foam, both twice.

Cut the fleur-de-lis (lily) decoration out of 6mm EVA foam twice.

Cut the rondel out of the 6mm EVA foam twice.

Cut the straps for the pauldrons out of 6mm EVA foam twice and the strap for the gorget back once.

Cut eight (½-inch [1.5-cm]-diameter) circles out of 2mm EVA foam.

Cut the Velcro into three equal pieces. Mine ended up being 1½ inches (4 cm) long each.

Take some measurements to find out if the template for the gorget needs to be adjusted. Measure around your neck, and add 1 inch (2.5 cm) to this measurement for wearing ease. Using the template as is will result in a gorget that is 13½ inches (34 cm) wide on the top. If that is bigger than the measurement you took, then you can use the template as is, and the gorget should fit. But if your measurement is higher, adjust the template. Determine how much more width you need and divide that by four. Now add that width to both the *middle front* and the *middle back* of the templates. If you are unsure, make the gorget bigger. It is not comfortable if this piece is too small because it's worn around your neck.

Cut the gorget front, side and back pieces out of 6mm EVA foam twice (once mirrored).

BUILDING THE PAULDRON UPPER LAYER

1. Close the darts on both of the upper pauldron side pieces with the contact cement. This dart will help give the pauldron a rounded shape on the side so it fits nicely on the shoulders.

2. Glue the upper pauldron center piece to one of the side pieces. Use the registration marks as a guide for connecting the pieces.

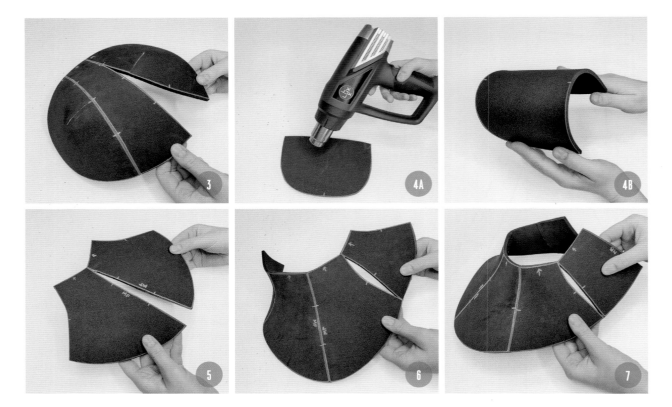

3. Glue the mirrored side piece to the other side of the center
piece, using the registration marks as a guide. Now the
upper layer for the pauldrons is assembled. Repeat steps 1, 2
and 3 for the other pauldron upper layer.

BUILDING THE MIDDLE AND BOTTOM LAYERS

4. Heat the two middle layer pieces and two bottom layer
pieces for the shoulder armor with the heat gun. When the
foam is hot, shape the pieces so they will be round. Hold the
pieces for a few minutes until they cool down, so the foam
will hold the new shape.

BUILDING THE GORGET BASE

5. Glue the two pieces for the front of the gorget together,
using the registration marks as a guide for connecting
the pieces.

6. Glue the side piece to the front piece of the gorget. Use
the registration marks as a guide for connecting the pieces.
Also glue the other side part to the other side of the gorget.

7. Glue the back piece to the side piece of the gorget. Use the
registration marks as a guide for connecting the pieces. Also
glue the other back piece to the other side of the gorget.
Now the base shape of the gorget is assembled.

**Note: Be careful not to close up the gorget by gluing it
together on the middle back. The middle back needs to
stay open.**

8. Heat the gorget base with the heat gun. When the foam is hot, you can shape it so it will be rounder. Also try to curve the top and bottom of the middle front a bit outwards so it will be more comfortable to wear around the neck. Hold the piece for a few minutes until it cools down and the foam holds the new shape. If you don't feel comfortable creating the rondels and the details on the armor pieces, then just craft the base shapes and the straps for the attachments and leave the details out. It will still look really cool! If you choose this, continue with step 22 now.

DECORATING THE EDGES OF THE PAULDRON UPPER LAYER

9. Hold the ½-inch (1-cm)-wide strip of 2mm EVA foam to the edges of the pauldron, mark how long it should be to cover the full edge of the pauldron piece and cut it to the right size. You will need one continuous piece of edging for the pauldron upper layer.

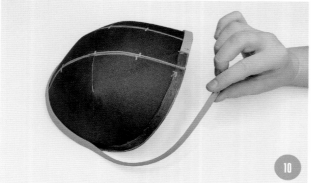

10. Glue the strip of foam on the pauldron all around the edge using the contact cement. Glue where the two ends of the foam strip meet, creating a continuous edge. Repeat these steps for the second shoulder.

DECORATING THE EDGES OF THE MIDDLE AND BOTTOM LAYER

11. Hold the ½-inch (1-cm)-wide strip of 2mm EVA foam to the edges of the middle and bottom layer pieces, mark how long the edge should be to cover the edges of these pieces (leaving the top edge free) and cut it to the right lengths. You will end up with four pieces of edging—one for each layer piece.

12. Glue the strips of foam on the pauldron layers around the edges using the contact cement.

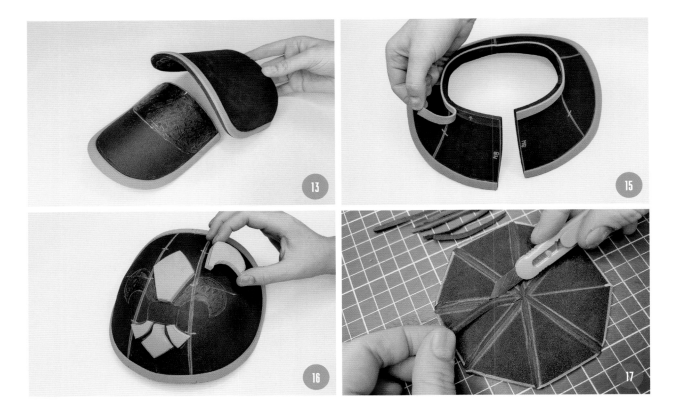

13. Place the middle layer on top of the bottom layer and decide how much you want the bottom layer to stick out from underneath. Mark with a paint marker where they overlap. Now apply a thin layer of contact cement to both the top layer and the middle layer, and when the glue is tacky, press the two layers together firmly. Repeat for the other pauldron.

DECORATING THE EDGES OF THE GORGET

14. Measure the ½-inch (1-cm)-wide strip of 2mm EVA foam to the top and bottom edges of the gorget, and cut it to the right lengths to cover the edges. You will end up with two pieces of edging—one for the top and one for the bottom.

15. Glue the strips of foam to the gorget top and bottom edge, using the contact cement.

ADDING THE LILIES TO THE PAULDRON UPPER LAYER

16. Glue the petals of the lily decoration to the pauldron, using the contact cement. Set the two middle pieces of the lily aside for now, but glue these two on top of each other to get a double-thick piece of foam. Repeat this on the other pauldron and try to make it as symmetrical as possible.

MAKING THE RONDEL

17. Place the rondel piece upside down on the cutting mat. Mark the lines for the undercuts that are shown on the template. On those lines, make V-shaped cuts in the foam with a sharp craft knife. Make sure not to cut all the way through the foam. Put the material you cut away aside. On page 19 you can read more about making undercuts in foam.

18. In between the grooves that you just cut, make straight cuts. Don't cut all the way down to the center of the shape, but only about 75 percent.

19. Add some contact cement inside the V-shaped grooves. When the glue is tacky, fold the grooves closed. This creates nice ridges on the top side of the foam.

20. Add some contact cement inside the remaining cuts. Don't wait too long now, because the glue still needs to be wet for the next bit. Take the material that you cut out in step 17, crack the slits open and put the material inside. This will make the cuts stand open.

21. While the foam piece may look messy on the bottom, when you flip it around, you will notice that it looks super neat on the front! It looks like a three-dimensional star. Repeat these steps for the other rondel.

PREPARING THE STRAPS

22. Take the three 6mm EVA foam straps and glue the 2mm EVA foam circles on them, using the contact cement. These circles resemble rivets.

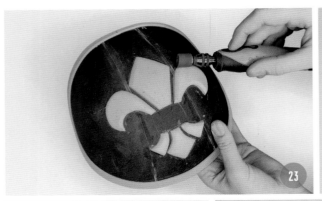

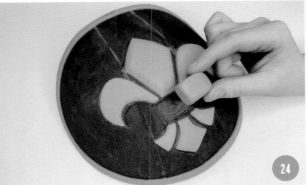

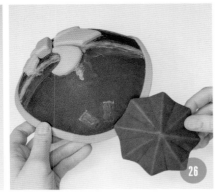

CLEANING UP THE EDGES

23. Use the rotary tool with a sanding drum attached to it (120-grit) to sand the edges of the pauldron pieces, the rondels and the gorget. The transition between the glued-on edges and the armor pieces will get super smooth in this step. Also sand the glue seams and the edges of the lily decoration.

Sand the double-layered middle of the lily detail. Only sand the sides and the top, and leave the bottom flat. Lastly, also sand the edges and the rivets on the three straps smooth. The result of the sanding will look nicest when using a rotary tool, but you can also use regular sandpaper. After the sanding is done, clean the foam pieces by removing all of the dust.

24. Glue the smoothed-out lily middle pieces to the pauldrons to finish the decoration.

OPTIONAL: SMOOTHING SEAMS WITH FILLER

25. This step is optional, and you can do this to hide the glue seams from assembling the armor pieces even more. If these seams are already nicely smooth from the sanding, simply skip this step.

For smoothing the seams, apply some filler on the seams and smooth it out after adding some water to it (page 23). Leave the filler to dry overnight, and add more layers if necessary.

ADDING THE RONDELS

26. Glue the rondels to the front of the pauldrons.

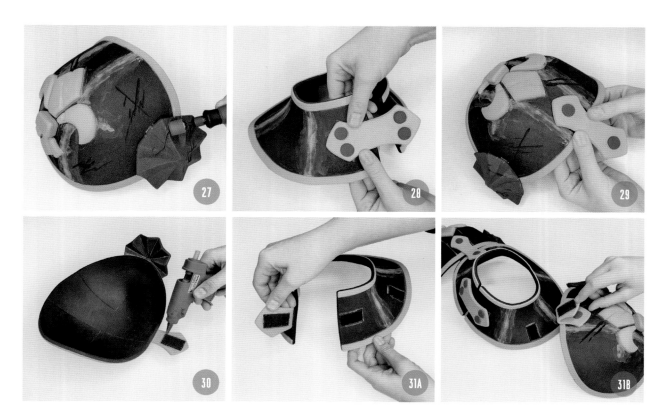

OPTIONAL: CREATING BATTLE DAMAGE

27. If you want to add battle damage to the pauldrons and gorget, review the technique on page 24.

MAKE IT WEARABLE

28. Glue the wide strap on only one end of the gorget.

29. Glue the thinner straps to both of the pauldrons.

30. Mark the bottom of the foam straps where the three hook pieces of the Velcro need to be attached. Turn the hot glue gun on. When the tool is ready to use, apply some hot glue to one of the marked spots and press the hook piece of the Velcro firmly on there. Now apply a thin layer of hot glue around the Velcro and make sure to cover the edges a bit. This will make it more secure. Repeat this for the other straps. Leave the glue to cool for 10 minutes before continuing to the next step.

31. Push the straps with the Velcro firmly into the foam where it will need to go so that it leaves a visible mark pressed into the foam. Quickly mark with a paint marker so that you know where the corresponding loop piece of the Velcro needs to go. Then take the hot glue gun and apply some hot glue on one of the marked spots and press the loop piece of the Velcro firmly on there. Apply a thin layer of hot glue around the Velcro and make sure to cover the edges a bit. Repeat this for the rest of the pieces.

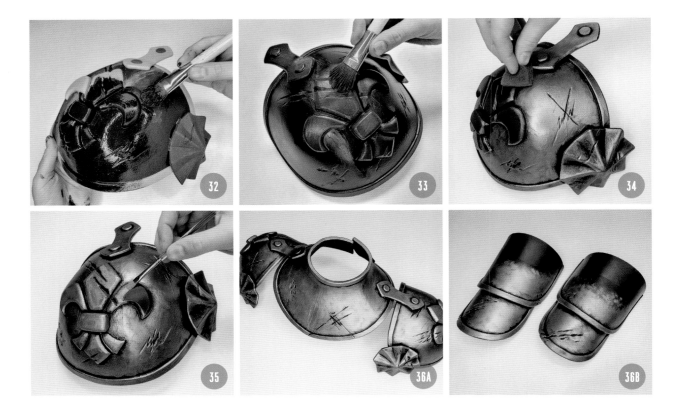

PRIMING AND PAINTING

32. Prepare the pieces for priming and painting by heat-sealing them with the heat gun. When the foam is cooled down, apply a flexible primer onto the pauldrons, arm layers and gorget. Cover the complete front of the pieces and also a little bit on the inside (about 1 inch [2.5 cm]). Use as many coats of primer as needed until you like how the surface looks. I used two layers of HexFlex black. Leave the primer to dry for 2 to 4 hours.

33. Apply some dark brown acrylic paint on the lily decorations. This will serve as a good shadow color for the gold. Leave it to dry for 2 to 4 hours.

34. Apply silver acrylic paint on the armor pieces. (I used Dark Silver from HexFlex.) Dab it on with a sponge instead of a brush to prevent brushstrokes. Put only a little bit of paint on the sponge each time and try to stay away from the corners and the battle damage dents so the black shadow color will still show through, creating more depth. If you managed to keep the shadows dark, and get a nice gradient in this step already, you can skip adding the oil paint in step 36. Acrylic metallic paint usually dries really quickly, so leave it to dry for 1 hour.

35. Apply gold metallic acrylic paint on the lily decorations. (I used 14kg Gold from Cospaint.) Only paint the raised surface and not the shadows to give it even more depth. Leave it to dry for 1 hour.

36. **Optional:** Take your paint job to the next level by creating even more shadows with black oil paint (page 32). In the example project, I skipped this step because the shadows were already looking good. Finish by protecting your project with a layer of varnish (page 32). For this project, I recommend coating the whole piece with satin acrylic varnish.

Note: If you applied the oil paint shadows, go for the spray varnish to coat the whole piece. Oil paint dries very slowly and it can take multiple weeks to dry. Using a brush could smear the oil paint in this step.

37A

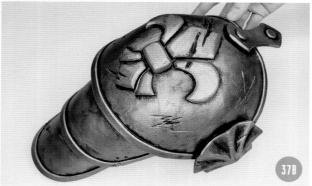

37B

FINAL ASSEMBLY

37. Place the arm layers underneath the pauldron and see where you want them to sit. Now mark it on the inside of the pauldron with a paint marker. Take two of the little strips of the 2mm EVA foam. Apply a thin layer of contact cement to the layers, and to the places where you will connect the arm layers to the pauldron. When the glue is tacky, press the strips of foam firmly on the armor, connecting the armor parts. Now the layers are connected underneath the pauldrons, but they can still move.

The shoulder armor with gorget can now be worn by putting the gorget around the neck and fastening it on the back with the Velcro. Then the pauldrons can be attached to the gorget with the Velcro.

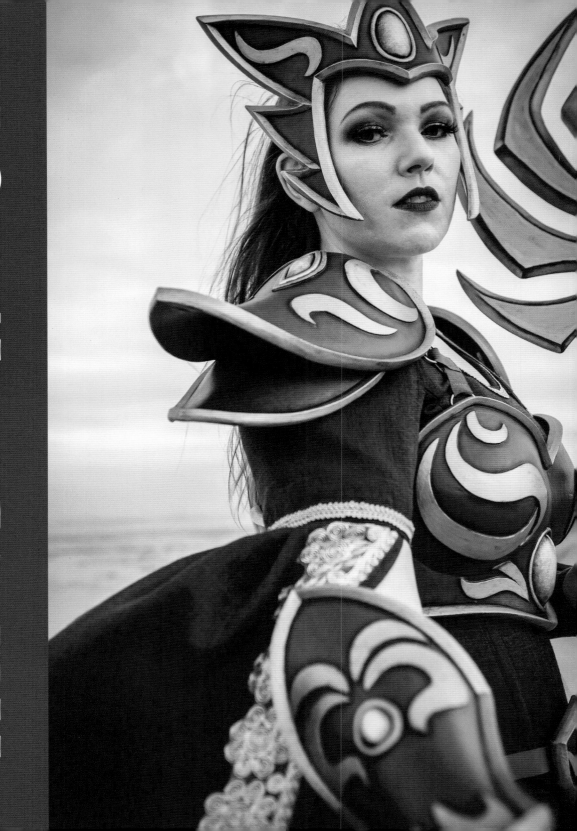

ARM AND
HAND ARMOR

MATERIALS

Layered Elven Bracers templates (digital pattern)

1 (12 x 9-inch [30 x 23-cm]) sheet of 6mm EVA foam

Contact cement

32 inches (80 cm) of EVA foam prefab half-round dowel (I used 5mm wide)

Foam clay

Flexible primer (black)

Acrylic paint (dark brown, light brown)

Wax paint (I used Rub 'n Buff gold) or metallic acrylic paint

Matte and glossy varnish (optional)

2 thin strips of jersey fabric (moss green)

TOOLS

Paint marker

Craft knife

Cutting mat

Heat gun

Safety tools, including a respirator, dust mask and safety glasses (review page 16)

Rotary tool with sanding drum (120-grit), or regular sandpaper

Belt puncher or hole puncher

Scissors

Wooden clay modeling tool

Brushes, sponge and a piece of cloth for painting

LAYERED ELVEN BRACERS
With Golden Leaves

These layered vambraces (arm guards) look like they are made out of leather, but of course they are EVA foam! The brown base color and fine golden leaf decorations make these armor pieces very fitting for a wood elf character. The elegant leaves are sculpted with foam clay so they weigh next to nothing. Painted with gilding wax, the branches look like they were forged out of antique precious metals. To make these comfortable to wear, we'll use some elastic fabric lacing in a matching color to make them close around the arms without hurting.

PREPARATION

Use your template to trace and cut the wrist piece (layer 1) out of the 6mm EVA foam four times (twice mirrored). When cutting these, make sure to cut all the edges at an inward angle (page 18).

Cut layers 2, 3 and 4 out of 6mm EVA foam twice. (These won't need to be mirrored because the pieces are symmetrical.) When cutting these layers, cut all the edges at an inward angle. This will help with the final look of the bracers.

BUILDING THE WRIST PART (LAYER 1)

1. Apply a thin layer of contact cement to the middle edges of the left and right piece for the wrist part. When the glue is tacky, connect the two pieces to form the wrist part of the bracers. Repeat this step for the other bracer too.

SHAPING LAYERS 2 TO 4

2. Place bracer layers 2, 3 and 4 on the cutting mat, upside down. Make a V-shaped cut across the middle. Make sure not to cut all the way through the foam, only about 75 percent of the way through. Remove the material that you cut away.

3. Apply a bit of contact cement in the groove and when the glue is tacky, fold the foam so the groove closes. Now on the other side, a straight ridge will have formed. Repeat these steps for both bracers (six times total).

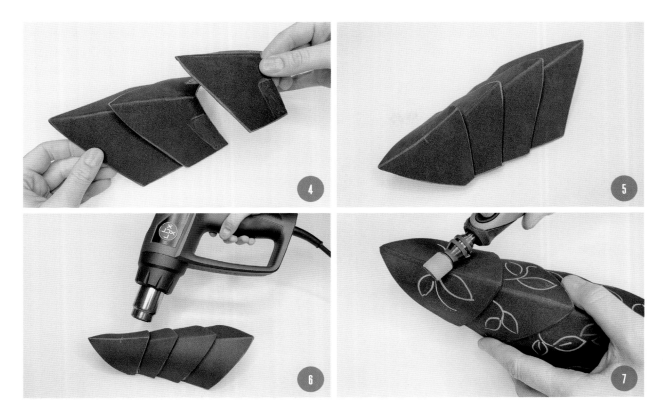

STACKING THE LAYERS

4. Stack the four layers for each bracer and see how they fit on your arm. Decide where you want the pieces to be attached and mark the glue points with a paint marker so you know where to apply the glue. Apply a thin layer of contact cement to the underside of the top layer and the outside of the under layer. Only apply the glue on the sides, and not over the whole layer (see image).

5. When the glue is tacky, press the layers of foam on top of each other. Repeat this until the full bracer is formed. Repeat these steps for the other bracer.

HEAT-SHAPING

6. Heat the bracer with the heat gun. When the foam is hot, you can shape it so it is more rounded. Be careful that the foam is not too hot, since you will be shaping it on your arm. When the bracer is in the desired shape, hold it for a few

minutes until it is cooled down. Then the foam will stay in its new shape. Repeat with the other bracer. If you want to add the leaf details like described in steps 9 through 12, also draw the design for those on the bracers with a paint marker.

If you don't like the leaves on the bracers or don't feel ready to do the sculpting yet, you can simply leave them out. The bracers will also look really cool without the decorations. And when you feel more advanced, you can add the sculpted leaves.

OPTIONAL: CLEANING UP THE EDGES

7. Skip this step if you already like how the edges of the foam look. Using the rotary tool with 120-grit sanding drum, sand the edges of the bracer until they're smooth. The result of the sanding will look nicest when using a rotary tool, but you can also use regular sandpaper for this job. After the sanding is done, clean the foam piece by removing all of the dust.

MAKE HOLES

8. Mark four spots on each side of the bracer to make holes. Using the belt puncher or hole puncher, punch holes through the foam. Make sure to leave some foam around the holes to make it less prone to ripping once the armor piece is being laced up.

ADD STEMS AND FOAM CLAY LEAVES

9. Take the 5mm half-round dowel and lay it on your stem markings to see how long the pieces need to be and cut them to size. To make the tips pointy, cut them with a pair of scissors. Mark the bottom of the dowels with letters to prevent mixing them up when gluing them to the foam.

10. Apply a thin layer of contact cement to the bottom of the dowels and on the lines where they need to go on the armor. When the glue is tacky, press the dowels on the armor pieces. Make sure that the pointy ends are pointing upwards (towards the widest part of the bracer). After you've laid them all down, heat the armor with the heat gun to close the pores of the foam.

11. Take a bit of foam clay out of the pot and form a small flat leaf shape with it. If the foam clay is too dry, mix some water into it. Using your fingers, apply a little bit of water on the bracer where you want to place the leaf. This will make the foam clay stick better to the foam. Then place the leaf shape on the bracer and press it down a bit. Repeat this step for as many leaves as you want on both armor pieces.

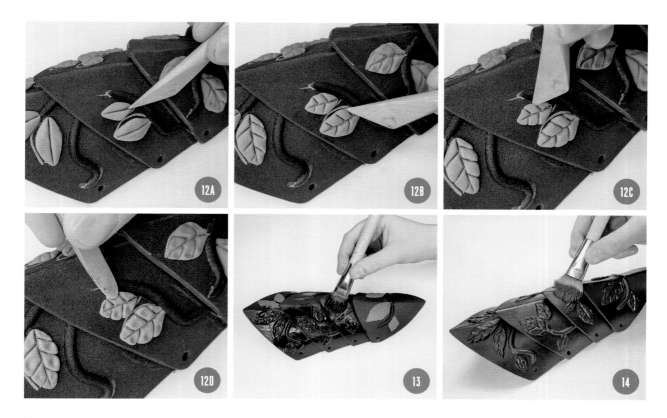

12. Carve lines in the leaves to look like veins with the wooden clay modeling tool. Push the foam clay back a bit on the sides to make a bit of a scalloped edge. Exaggerate this effect by pushing outwards softly on the leaves with a rounder wooden clay modeling tool. Now set the project aside for 24 to 48 hours so the foam clay can air-dry.

PRIMING AND PAINTING

13. Apply a flexible primer to both pieces. Cover the complete front of each piece and a bit of the inside too (about 1 inch [2.5 cm]). I used two layers of HexFlex black. Leave the primer to dry for 2 to 4 hours.

14. Apply a layer of brown acrylic paint on the bracers. Add more paint to the raised parts and less paint on the edges where shadows naturally occur. If your primer wasn't black, you can also add some black paint to the shadow parts. Leave the brown paint to dry for 2 to 4 hours.

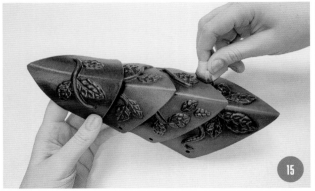

15. Take a lighter shade of brown or mix it by adding some white paint to the brown from the last step and apply some highlights. For this layer, I used a sponge to apply the paint, and I only used a little bit of paint on the sponge to create nice gradients. Add more paint on the raised parts to create even more depth. Leave the highlight layer of paint to dry for 1 to 2 hours.

16. To get a beautiful golden color on the stems and leaves, apply some gilding wax like Rub 'n Buff. I used the color Grecian Gold by Rub 'n Buff for this project. Just apply the waxy paint onto the foam with an old piece of cloth. Only paint the raised surface, and not the shadows, to give it more depth. The gilding wax doesn't need much time to dry, so you can continue immediately with the next step. If you can't find gilding wax, you can use metallic acrylic paint.

17. To protect the paint job, paint or spray the whole piece with a matte acrylic varnish. In this example, I used a brush-on acrylic varnish. Leave the varnish to dry for 2 to 4 hours.

18. This step is optional, but if you want the leaves to look more like real shiny metal, apply a layer of glossy varnish on the leaves and stems with a brush. Leave the whole paint job to dry overnight before continuing to the next step.

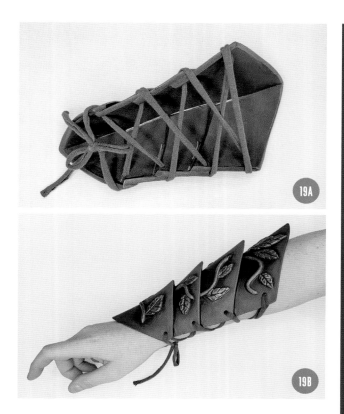

19A

19B

Get Creative! Ideas for Variations

Make the bracers look even more like leather by adding texture to the foam. One way is to use a rolled-up ball of aluminum foil to "stamp" a leather texture in the foam after it's been heated up with a heat gun. And another way is to use a rough sponge to apply the second layer of primer and work messy. That way you'll get texture on the foam that can make it look like leather.

If you want the bracers to look like metal instead of leather, paint them with a metallic color instead of brown. Add edges of thin strips of 2mm EVA foam around the layers to give it some extra detail.

You can wear the bracers over arm warmers to make it more comfortable against the skin. Simply buy arm warmers or sew them with a piece of elastic fabric.

In the example, the bracers are closed by lacing them up with stretchy material, but you can also glue straps with Velcro or buckles to them for the attachments. Or hot glue some Velcro to the underside of the bracers and attach them to a piece of clothing.

MAKE IT WEARABLE

19. Loop the strips of jersey fabric through the holes in the bracers to serve as lacing. Don't lace it too tight, because the material is foam after all, and it could rip from too much pressure.

Because of the stretchy laces, the armor pieces will be comfortable to wear.

MATERIALS

Dignified Bracers templates (pattern sheet VI)

1 (16 x 12-inch [40 x 30-cm]) sheet of 6mm EVA foam

1 (8 x 6-inch [20 x 15-cm]) piece of 2mm EVA foam

1 (8-inch [20-cm]) piece of ¾-inch (2-cm)-wide Velcro

Contact cement

60 inches (1.5 m) of EVA foam prefab triangular bevel (I used 10mm wide, high profile)

8 inches (20 cm) of EVA foam prefab half-round dowel (I used 5mm wide)

Foam clay

2 arm warmers

Filler (optional)

Hot glue stick

Flexible primer (black)

Acrylic paint (dark brown, metallic purple, pearl, gold and silver)

Black oil paint (optional)

Satin and glossy (spray) varnish (optional)

Fabric glue

DIGNIFIED BRACERS
With Swirls and Gems

These purple and gold bracers are elegantly shaped to enhance the silhouette of your armor and are perfect for a stylish spell-casting character. Pearlescent gems are the shiny centerpieces of these bracers, framed with swirly, gold detailing. In this project, we'll be adding some arm warmers so these beautiful bracers stay on almost like magic (perfect for a sorceress, right!?). This is such a convenient way to wear vambraces if you don't want visible attachments. The edges of these armor pieces are decorated with EVA foam prefabs. Prefabs are such a time-saver and will make any piece look amazing. Once you try them, you'll want to stick them on everything because they are so convenient.

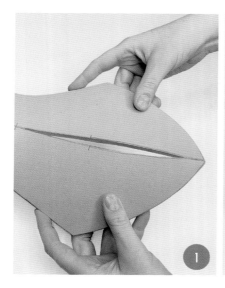 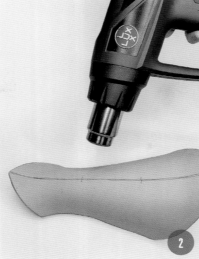

TOOLS

Paint marker

Craft knife

Cutting mat

Heat gun

Safety tools, including a respirator, dust mask and safety glasses (review page 16)

Rotary tool with sanding drum (120-grit) or regular sandpaper

Wooden clay modeling tool (optional)

Brushes for painting

Hot glue gun

Needle and thread

PREPARATION

Use your template to trace and cut the bracer base out of the 6mm EVA foam four times (twice mirrored).

Cut out the swirly details four times (twice mirrored) from the 2mm EVA foam.

Cut the Velcro in half so you have two equal pieces.

BUILDING THE BASE PIECES

1. Apply a thin layer of contact cement on both top edges of the bracer base pieces. When the glue is tacky, connect both halves of the bracer together. Use the registration marks as a guide. Repeat this step for the second bracer.

SHAPING THE BRACERS

2. After the glue has fully set, heat one armor piece with the heat gun. When the foam is hot, shape it to be rounded so it fits over your arm. Be careful that the foam is not too hot when you do this. When you like the shape, also curl up the front and back edges a little bit to create an interesting silhouette. Hold the armor piece for a few minutes in the desired shape until it's cooled down, so the foam will stay in this shape. Repeat this step for the second bracer. If you want to keep the bracers simple and don't want to add decorative edges and more detailing, continue now with step 5.

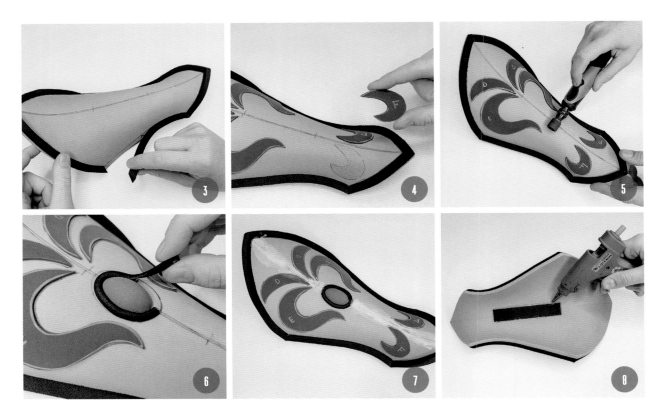

DECORATING THE BRACERS

3. Lay the triangular shaped bevel along the edges of the bracer to measure it, cut it to the right lengths, then glue the pieces on with the contact cement. Remember to cut the ends diagonally for nice pointy corners. Repeat this for the other bracer. For these bracers, you should have 12 pieces of prefab bevels in total (6 for each bracer).

4. Take the 12 swirly detail pieces (6 for each bracer) and glue those on both of the bracers.

CLEANING UP THE EDGES

5. Using the rotary tool with 120-grit sanding drum, sand the edges of the bracers smooth. The transition between the glued-on bevels and the armor pieces will get super smooth in this step. Also sand the glue seams smooth. The result of the sanding will look nicest when using a rotary tool, but you can also use regular sandpaper for this job. After the sanding is done, clean the foam pieces by removing all of the dust.

CREATING FAUX GEMSTONES

6. To create faux gemstones for each bracer, follow steps 6 and 7 for the Royal Headpiece (page 39).

OPTIONAL: SMOOTHING SEAMS WITH FILLER

7. If your seams are already nice and smooth from the sanding, skip this step. For smoothing the seams, apply some filler on the seams and smooth it out after adding some water to it (page 23). Leave the filler to dry overnight, and add more layers if necessary.

ADDING VELCRO

8. Place one hook part of a cut piece of Velcro on the underside of the bracer, in the middle, and mark the spot with a paint marker. Turn the hot glue gun on. When the tool is ready to use, apply some hot glue to the marked spot and firmly press the hook piece of the Velcro on. Now apply a thin layer of hot glue around the Velcro edges to make it more secure. Repeat for both bracers

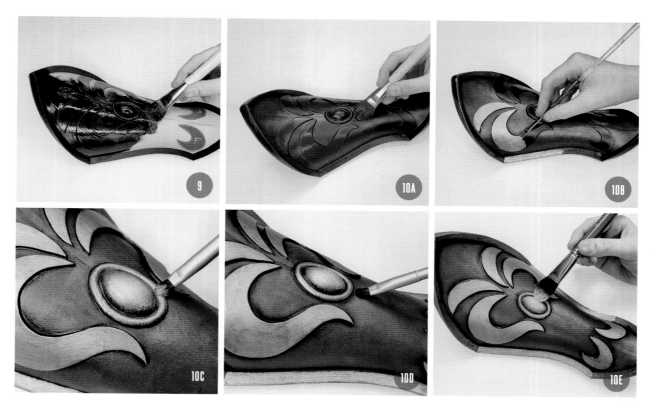

PRIMING AND PAINTING

9. Prepare the piece for priming and painting by heat-sealing it with the heat gun. When the foam is cool again, apply a flexible primer to the bracers. Cover the complete outside of the pieces and also a large part of the underside, because that will show when the armor piece is worn—especially the part at the elbow. I used two layers of HexFlex black. Let the primer dry for 2 to 4 hours.

10. To paint the bracers and finish the paint job, use the same technique that's described in steps 10 through 15 for the Royal Headpiece (pages 40 and 41).

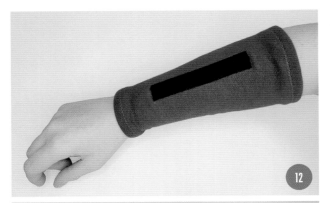

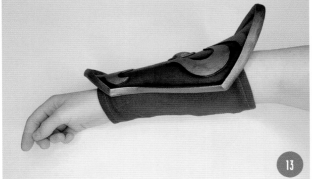

Get Creative! Ideas for Variations

Personalize the bracers by designing your very own details. And what about creating a cool texture on the bracers by gluing on layers of foam scales? Painted in a red or green color, these would make epic bracers for a dragon knight character.

If the purple and gold doesn't fit your character, use other colors. If you are making these for a spell-casting character, what kind of spells do they cast? Adjust the color scheme to fit better with the elemental spells from their arsenal, like fireballs (red, orange, gold) or water spells (blue, teal, silver).

Change the shape of the gems or add even more to each bracer. You could also use store-bought acrylic cabochons to make the gems if you don't want to use foam clay. Those come in various colors, shapes and sizes and are translucent.

Feel free to use other materials and techniques to create the attachments, like straps with Velcro or buckles. If you punch holes in the sides of the bracers, you can also lace them up to wear them.

MAKE IT WEARABLE

11. Place the loop part of the Velcro on the hook part that is glued on the bottom of the bracer so the harsh hook part won't damage the fabric of the arm warmer. Put one of the arm warmers on your arm. Place the bracer on the arm warmer and decide where you want to fix it to the arm warmer.

12. Pull the loop part of the Velcro off the bracer and with some fabric glue, attach it to the arm warmer. Wait for 10 minutes, or until the glue is dry, and then sew the Velcro to the fabric arm warmer with some stitches using needle and thread.

13. Now the bracers can be worn by first putting the arm warmers on your arms and then pushing the bracers on top of them. The Velcro will keep them in place.

HEROIC HEAVY ARM ARMOR

With a Knight's Crest

Unlike the other projects in this chapter, this armor wraps around the whole arm. The lower and upper pieces connect to each other with Velcro that is glued to the foam, making it super convenient to put these armor pieces on and take them off again. The lower piece is made from two pattern pieces that have slightly curved edges to give the final piece a more organic shape and a better fit. On the top of these bracers, a magnificent coat of arms shines: the golden lily.

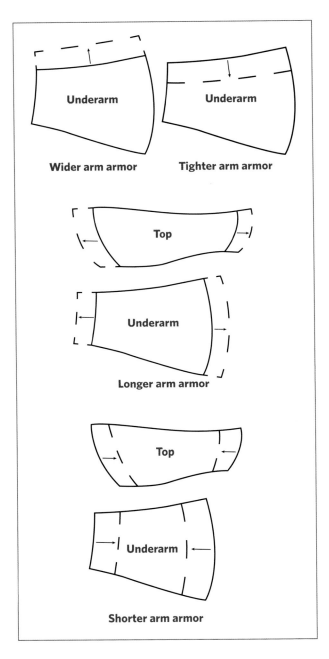

Wider arm armor

Tighter arm armor

Top

Underarm

Longer arm armor

Top

Underarm

Shorter arm armor

PREPARATION

Take some measurements to see if the arm armor will fit or if you need to make some adjustments to the template. If you intend to wear a sleeve underneath the armor, make sure to wear that while measuring. Measure around your wrist and around the largest part of your forearm and write these measurements down.

The template will work for a wrist that is 6 to 8 inches (15 to 20 cm) in diameter. The template will work for 10 to 13½ inches (25 to 34 cm) in diameter for the biggest part of the forearm. If your arm measurements fall between these ranges, then the bracers will fit using the template as is. If your arm is bigger, add extra width to the underarm pattern piece so the finished armor will be able to wrap around a bigger arm. If your arm is thinner, take away some width from the underarm pattern piece.

The finished armor piece is 6½ inches (17 cm) long on the bottom and 8¼ inches (21 cm) on the top. If you want it to be longer or shorter, add or take away length from the pattern pieces.

After you've made the necessary adjustments, use your templates to trace and cut the bracer base (top) out of 6mm EVA foam four times (twice mirrored).

Cut the arm armor base (underarm) out of 6mm EVA foam four times (twice mirrored).

Cut the pieces for the lily decorations out of 6mm EVA foam twice (one lily for each arm).

Cut the Velcro in four equal pieces.

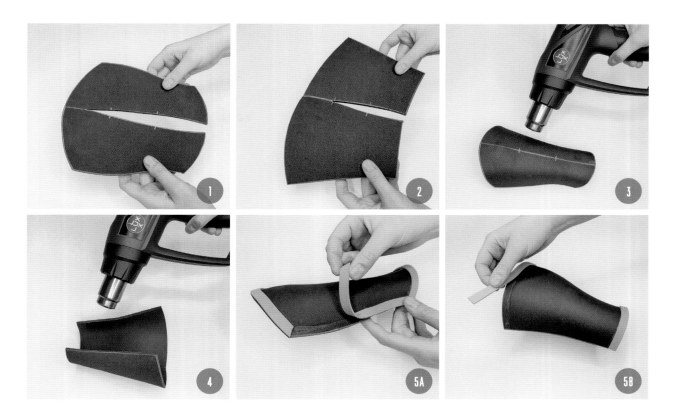

BUILDING THE BASE SHAPES

1. Apply a thin layer of contact cement on both top edges of the bracer top pieces. When the glue is tacky, connect both halves of the bracer top together, using the registration marks as a guide.

2. Apply a thin layer of contact cement to both top edges of the underarm base pieces. When the glue is tacky, connect both halves of the underarm base together, using the registration marks as a guide.

3. Heat the bracer top with the heat gun. When the foam is hot, you can shape it to be more rounded and fit well on top of your arm. Be careful that the foam is not too hot when you are shaping this piece on your arm. Hold the foam in the correct shape for a few minutes, or until it has cooled down. It will now hold its new shape.

4. Heat the underarm part with the heat gun. When the foam is hot, you can shape it to be more rounded and fit well, wrapped around your arm (the opening is on the top of your arm). Be careful that the foam is not too hot when you are shaping this piece. Hold the foam in the correct shape for a few minutes, or until it has cooled down. It will now hold its new shape. Repeat steps 1 through 4 for the second bracer. If you want to keep it simple, you can skip the decorations and continue with step 7 now.

DECORATING THE BRACERS

5. Measure, cut and glue the ½-inch (1-cm)-wide strip of 2mm EVA foam along the edges of the arm armor. On the top piece of the armor, add strips along the entire edge. In order to achieve pointy corners, make sure to cut the ends diagonally. The corners are not super sharp at the tips at the wrist or elbow, so you can follow those curves with a single piece of foam strip. You will end up with four pieces of edging for each top piece.

For the underarm piece, only add the strips along the edges at the wrist and elbow. You should end up with two pieces of edging for each underarm part. Repeat these steps for the other bracer.

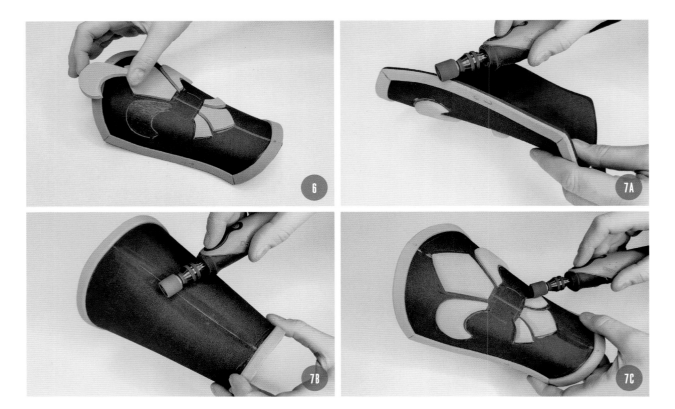

6. Glue the petals of the lily decoration to the top of one of the bracers. Repeat this on the other bracer and try to make it as symmetrical as possible. Leave the two pieces for the middle of the lily set aside for now, but glue these two on top of each other to get a double-thick piece of foam.

CLEANING UP THE EDGES

7. Use the rotary tool with a sanding drum attached to it (120-grit) to sand the edges of the armor pieces smooth. The transition between the glued-on edges and the bracer itself will get super smooth in this step. Also sand the glue seams and the edges of the lily decoration smooth.

Sand the double-layered middle piece of the lily detail. Only sand the sides and the top, and leave the bottom flat. The result of the sanding will look nicest when using a rotary tool, but you can also use regular sandpaper for this job. Repeat this step for the other bracer. After the sanding is done, clean the foam pieces by removing all of the dust.

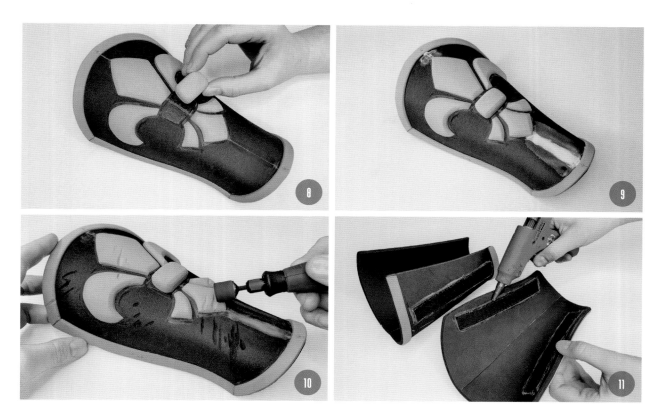

8. After everything is sanded, glue the smoothed-out lily middle to the bracer to finish the decoration. Repeat for the other bracer too.

OPTIONAL: SMOOTHING SEAMS WITH FILLER

9. If the seams are already smooth from the sanding, simply skip this step. For smoothing the seams, apply some filler on the seams and smooth it out after adding some water to it (page 23). Leave the filler to dry overnight, and add more layers if necessary.

CREATING BATTLE DAMAGE

10. If you want to add battle damage to the arm armor, review the technique on page 24. At this stage, prepare all four pieces for priming and painting by heat-sealing them with a heat gun.

MAKE THEM WEARABLE

11. Place two hook parts of the Velcro on both sides of the underside of the top part of the bracer, and mark the spots with a paint marker. Turn the hot glue gun on. When the tool is ready to use, apply some hot glue to the marked spots and firmly press the hook pieces of the Velcro on. Now apply a thin layer of hot glue around the Velcro edges to make it more secure. Repeat this for the other bracer. Leave the glue to cool for 10 minutes before continuing to the next step.

12. Now put the underarm part of the armor over your arm and close it on the top as much as possible. Take the top part of the bracer and push it firmly on the bottom part, making an impression on the foam with the "hooks" of the Velcro. Now you know where to place the loop part of the Velcro on the underarm part of the arm armor. Mark this spot with a paint marker. Then glue the Velcro on the foam like in the last step. Repeat this for the other bracer. Leave the glue to cool for 10 minutes before continuing to the next step.

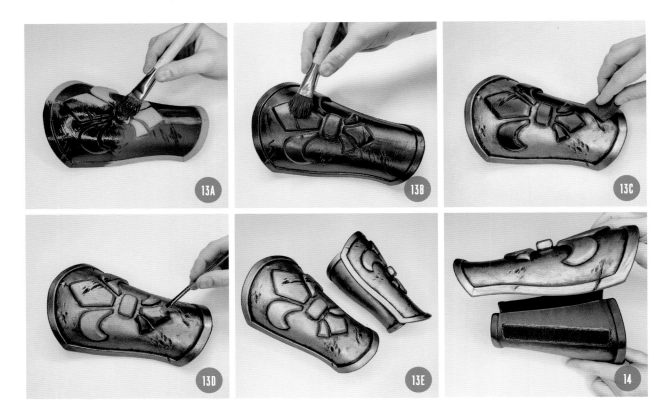

Note: You can try the armor on your arms to marvel at your work before painting! Isn't it cool how you made an armor piece that covers your full under arm? Great job!

PRIMING AND PAINTING

13. Prime, paint and, optionally, protect the paint job with some varnish by using the same technique from steps 32 through 36 from the Battleworn Shoulder Armor and Gorget project (page 80).

14. Now the arm armor pieces can be worn by first putting the bottom part under your arm and then pushing the upper part on top of it firmly. The Velcro will keep it tight.

Get Creative! Ideas for Variations

If you like the idea of having a piece of armor that fully wraps around your arm but don't really like the shape of this particular piece, you can swap the top part with a different bracer design.

Sketch your own coat of arms for your knight character and use that instead of the lilies in this example to make the armor piece more personalized. To make this arm armor fit for a king, change the color of the paint job from silver to gold to give it a royal feel.

Leave the 2mm EVA foam edging off if you want a cleaner-looking armor piece. When you want it to look brand new, skip the battle damage.

EPIC KNIGHT GAUNTLETS
With Armored Fingers

In this project, we're going to make hand and finger armor that can complement nearly any armor costume. There's a bigger piece of armor that sits on the hand, and the fingers are covered in tiny segments of 2mm EVA foam, looking like scales. Because those segments are all separate, there's lots of room for movement when wearing these armored gloves. By using store-bought gloves for this project, the daunting task of sewing your own gloves is taken away, making this project more beginner friendly. The gloves that I chose for this project are hand gloves made from soft sweater fabric, but you can also use longer gloves if that fits your character better. It's even possible to use pleather gloves if you like that look.

If you paint the foam in a common metal color like silver or gold, you will be able to wear them with multiple costumes. This way you won't need to craft a new pair of gauntlets for every costume, which saves time and money! When you are wearing these armored gloves, be careful not to damage them because the material is EVA foam, after all, and you're not wearing actual metal gauntlets. These foam ones are way more comfortable though.

MATERIALS

1 pair of fabric gloves

Epic Knight Gauntlets templates (digital pattern)

1 (12 x 8-inch [30 x 20-cm]) piece of 2mm EVA foam

Flexible primer (black)

Acrylic paint (silver)

Satin (spray) varnish (optional)

Painter's tape (optional)

Fabric glue

Latex or vinyl gloves (optional)

TOOLS

Paint marker

Scissors

Heat gun

Safety tools, including a respirator (review page 16)

Screwdriver (optional)

Thin PVC pipe (optional)

Brushes and sponges, for painting

101

PREPARATION

Find a pair of fabric gloves that fit you well. I chose a dark gray pair made out of stretchy and soft sweater fabric.

Because hand sizes are super personal and can be different for everyone, I tried to help a little by adding three size variations to the templates for this project. To determine which size you will need, check what size of glove you usually buy. Is it size S? Then use size S (small) of the template. If it is a size M, then use that size of template, and when it's L or XL, use the biggest version of the template.

Trace and cut all the pieces for the gauntlet out of 2mm thick foam twice (once mirrored for the other hand). Don't forget to mark all the pieces on the back to avoid mixing them up later.

SHAPING THE PIECES

1. Heat the gauntlet pieces with the heat gun. Because these pieces are rather small, I hold them softly onto the table with a screwdriver so the wind from the heat gun won't blow them away. When the foam is hot, you can shape it around your hand and fingers so the segments fit better. Be careful that the foam is not too hot, because it will be touching your hand and fingers while you are shaping it. Heat two or three segments at a time. If you try to heat too many, they will cool down before you get the chance to shape them all. The good news is you won't have to heat-seal the foam now, because you've basically already done that in this step by heating it up.

PRIMING AND PAINTING

2. Apply a flexible primer to all of the segments. Completely cover the front of the pieces. Use as many coats of primer as needed until you like how the surface looks. I used two layers of HexFlex black, but you can also use something else, like Plastidip or Flexbond. Leave the primer to dry for 2 to 4 hours.

Note: Because these shapes are so tiny, it can be a challenge to paint them while holding them with your hands. Instead, try adding a bit of painter's tape to the bottom of each segment, and use that to stick it onto a stick or piece of PVC pipe (see image 3). Doing that will also allow you to use a spray primer instead of a brush-on primer.

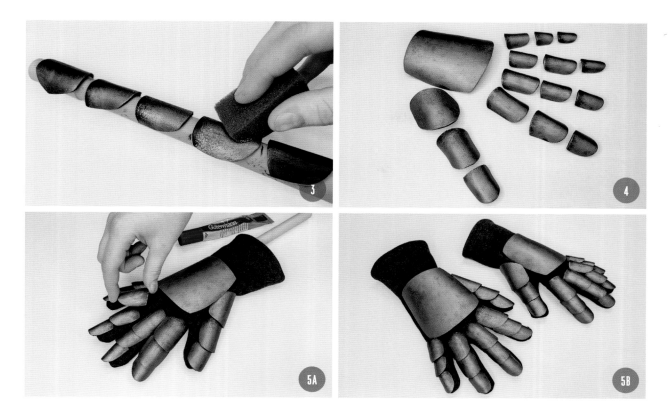

3. Apply silver acrylic paint on the armor pieces. (I used Dark Silver from HexFlex.) Dab it on with a sponge instead of a brush to prevent brushstrokes. Put only a little bit of paint on the sponge each time and try to create a bit of a gradient. Keep the tip that will point towards the wrist black, and make a silver gradient in the direction of the fingertips. This gradient is optional, but it will create more depth.

4. Leave the paint job to fully dry overnight and then optionally add a layer of varnish to protect it. Either spray or paint over the paint with a satin acrylic varnish. I used HexFlex Clear and applied one layer with a brush. Leave it to dry overnight.

ADD SEGMENTS TO THE GLOVES

5. With the fabric glue, attach the foam segments to the gloves starting from the tip of your fingers working toward your wrist. This is easiest when you wear the gloves, and to protect your skin, you can wear latex or vinyl gloves underneath the fabric gloves. Another option is to use the PVC pipe from earlier and put that inside the glove's finger you

are working on. It will mimic the round shape of a finger and can help with gluing the segments on. Leave the fabric glue to dry for 10 minutes before you glue on the next segment. Continue until all the segments are attached to the gloves.

Now the armored gloves/gauntlets are ready to wear with your costume!

Get Creative! Ideas for Variations

Instead of round segments, make them pointy, and they will look like epic dragon claws.

The 2mm foam that is used for this project is, of course, rather thin. But you can still use the undercut technique to cut little V-shaped grooves on the underside of each segment, right over the middle. Then apply a bit of contact cement in the groove and fold it closed. Now you get neat ridges on top of the segments, which add a whole new dimension to the gauntlets.

TORSO AND WAIST ARMOR

MAGICAL SORCERESS' BREASTPLATE

With a Shining Gemstone

This fierce breastplate sure has some curves going on—both in the shape and in the detailing. It looks beautiful with the whole Sorceress ensemble (see page 7) and works great when worn over a dress or even on a bare stomach as "bikini armor." The D-rings make it easy to lace the armor with either some elastic or ribbons. The Noble Layered Pauldrons (page 64) can be attached to the front of this breastplate to make them comfortable to wear.

This particular armor piece has a very feminine cut, so if you are looking for something more gender-neutral, I would suggest checking out the Knight Chestplate (page 114). You can still use the swirly decorations and foam clay gem from this project on that one though. Just do some mixing and matching with the templates and decorations from different projects to make it your own.

MATERIALS

Magical Sorceress' Breast-plate templates (pattern sheets III, IV and V)

1 (26 x 14–inch [65 x 35–cm]) sheet of 6mm EVA foam

1 (14 x 12–inch [35 x 30–cm]) piece of 2mm EVA foam

Contact cement

79 inches (2 m) of EVA foam prefab triangular bevel (I used 10mm wide, high profile)

10 inches (25 cm) of EVA foam prefab half-round dowel (I used 5mm wide)

Foam clay

Filler (optional)

6 metal D-rings (I used 1-inch [2.5-cm]-wide D-rings)

Elastic (purple)

1 (1½-inch [4-cm]) piece of ¾-inch (2-cm)-wide Velcro (purple)

Fabric glue (optional)

Flexible primer (black)

Acrylic paint (dark brown, metallic purple, pearl, gold and silver)

Oil paint (black) (optional)

Satin and glossy (spray) varnish (optional)

(continued)

Measuring tape

Paint marker

Craft knife

Cutting mat

Heat gun

Safety tools, including a respirator, dust mask and safety glasses (review page 16)

1 (5-inch [12-cm]-diameter) acrylic sphere (optional)

Rotary tool with sanding drum (120-grit), or regular sandpaper

Wooden clay modeling tool (optional)

Brushes for painting

A sewing machine, or needle and thread

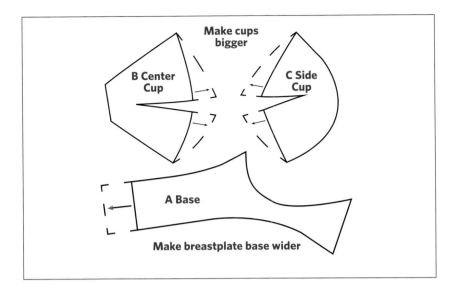

PREPARATION

Determine if the original template will fit you. Since this breastplate has a lace-up closure on the back, there is some wiggle room when it comes to size. Measure and write down your underbust circumference. The original template will result in a breastplate that would fit a minimum of a 30½-inch (77-cm) underbust and a cup size of A to C. Keep in mind that the total circumference of the breastplate base is 30½ inches (77 cm), and the extra width needed to close around your body will be open and covered by the lacing.

If your underbust circumference is less than 30½ inches (77 cm), then divide the difference by two and shorten the breastplate base pattern piece by that amount on both sides of the center back. If you want more open room at the back for the lace-up part, then take away even more.

If your underbust circumference is more than 35½ inches (90 cm), divide the excess amount by two and add that to the breastplate base pattern piece on both sides of the center back.

If your cup size is bigger than C, the cups of the original template will probably be too tight for you. To adjust these, add some width to the pattern pieces B (center cup) and C (side cup) in the middle of the cups. This can be a bit tricky to do if you haven't worked with patterns before.

It's hard to take measurements before crafting the breastplate to know how much elastic you will need. So I suggest crafting the breastplate, then try it out with some thread or string you have laying around to find out how long your piece of elastic needs to be.

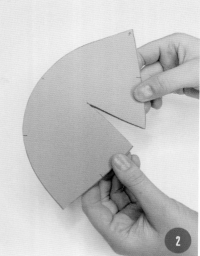

This is optional, but if you want to add the attachments for the Noble Layered Pauldrons (page 64), you will need an additional 7 inches (18 cm) of elastic and 1½ inches (4 cm) of extra Velcro.

Cut the breastplate base and the cup pieces B and C out of 6mm EVA foam twice (once mirrored). For the breastplate base piece, make sure to cut the part where the cups will be attached at a slight outward angle. The place where you need to cut at an angle is marked on the template.

Using the 2mm EVA foam, cut out the swirly details twice (once mirrored).

Cut six (2 x 1-inch [5 x 2.5-cm]) strips of 2mm EVA foam. These will be used to attach D-rings to the front and the back of the breastplate.

BUILDING THE BASE

1. Close the dart on the middle front cup piece (pattern piece B) using the contact cement.

2. Also close the dart on the side cup piece (pattern piece C). This dart will help give the cup a more rounded shape.

3. Glue both halves together along the middle edges. Use the registration marks as a guide for connecting the pieces. Repeat these steps for the second cup, which will be mirrored.

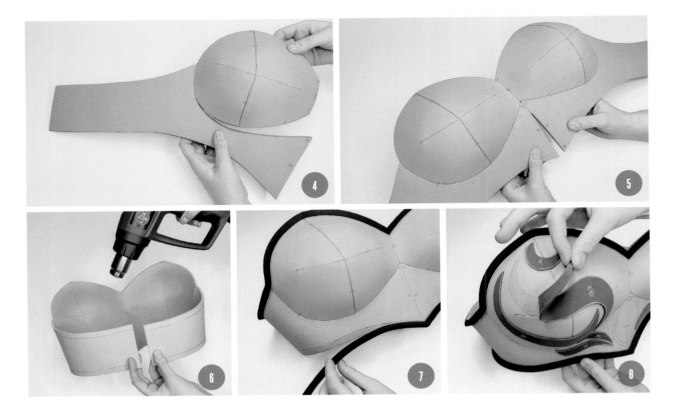

4. Glue the cup to the breastplate base (pattern piece A) on the part that was cut at an angle. Use the registration marks as a guide for connecting the pieces. Repeat this step for the other side.

5. Glue the two halves of the breastplate together along the middle front. The breastplate is now put together.

SHAPING THE BREASTPLATE

6. After the glue has fully set, heat the breastplate with the heat gun. When the foam is hot, you can shape it to better wrap around your body. Hold the armor piece for a few minutes in the desired shape until it's cooled down.

Pro Tip: You can put an acrylic sphere (found in craft stores) underneath the cups and press the foam cups on the outside with your hands, while the foam is still warm, to make the cups rounder and the darts and glue seams flatter and less visible.

If you don't feel comfortable creating the foam clay gems and the other details on the armor piece, skip steps 7, 8 and 10. It will still look really cool! If you feel more advanced, then just do all the steps to make the armor super detailed.

DECORATING THE BREASTPLATE

7. Measure, cut and glue the triangular-shaped bevels along the edges of the breastplate. In order to achieve nice pointy corners in the middle front of the bottom and top, make sure to cut the ends diagonally. You should end up with two pieces of bevel for the upper edge and two for the bottom edge of the breastplate.

8. Glue the ten swirly detail pieces to the breastplate base and on the cups. Try to make it as symmetrical as possible.

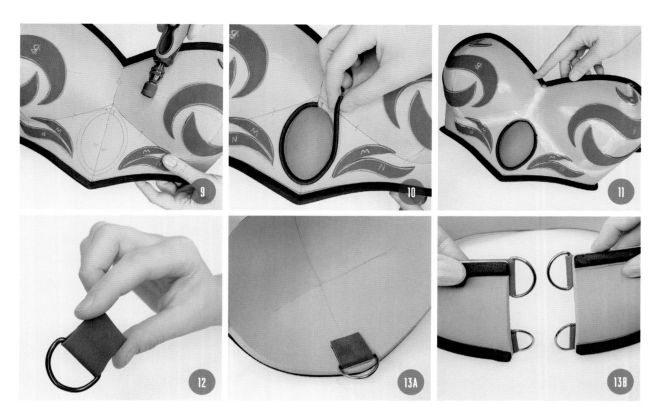

CLEANING UP THE EDGES

9. Using the rotary tool with 120-grit sanding drum, sand the edges of the breastplate and the glue seams smooth. The result of the sanding will look nicest when using a rotary tool, but you can also use regular sandpaper for this job. After the sanding is done, clean the foam piece by removing all of the dust.

CREATING FAUX GEMSTONES

10. To create a faux gemstone for the breastplate, follow steps 6 and 7 from the Royal Headpiece (page 39).

OPTIONAL: SMOOTHING SEAMS WITH FILLER

11. If your seams are already smooth from the sanding, skip this step. For smoothing the seams, apply filler on the seams and smooth it out after adding some water to it (page 23). Leave the filler to dry overnight, and add more layers if necessary.

ADDING D-RINGS

12. Apply contact cement to both ends of each of the 6 strips of 2mm EVA foam. When the glue is almost dry, fold the foam strips through the D-rings and press them closed so the metal rings are attached.

13. To attach the D-rings to the breastplate, glue the foam piece with the D-ring to the inside of the breastplate. Glue one D-ring at the top of each cup. And glue the other four D-rings to the middle back of the breastplate; two on each side. The D-rings will be used later to add elastic for wearing.

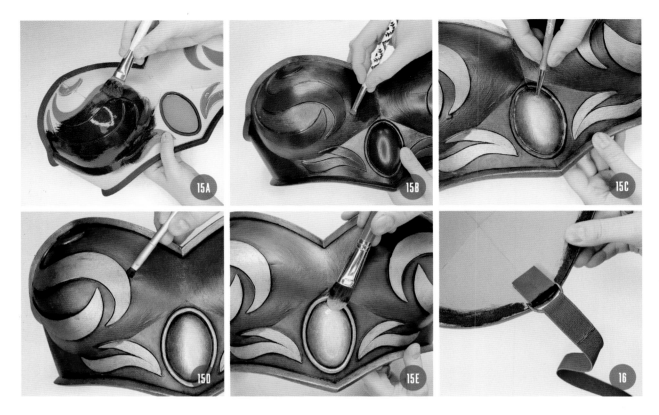

14. Measure how much elastic you will need to make the attachments for this breastplate. It will be helpful to ask a friend to help you for this step.

Take two pieces of string at least 4 feet (1.2 m) long, and tie each one to a D-ring on the front of the breastplate. Now try the breastplate on. Ask your friend to bring both strings over your shoulders and cross them behind your back. Then use the four D-rings on the middle back of the breastplate to lace the string like a corset, and end with two loose strings through the bottom D-rings. Tie those together in a bow and mark where they are tied. Now you can take the breastplate off, but make sure that you can still see where the strings are marked. For reference, see image 17 (page 111).

If you're using elastic for the final ties, remove 3 inches (8 cm) from your string measurement to compensate for its stretchiness. If you're using nonelastic ties, add 3 inches (8 cm) to the measurement for attaching it onto the breast-plate. For me, these pieces were both 32 inches (80 cm) long. In the end, you can still play around with the length of the

elastic and cut some off if they are too long. So it's better to have a bit too long elastic than too short.

PRIMING AND PAINTING

15. To prime, paint and, optionally, protect the breastplate, use the same technique that's described in steps 9 through 15 on the Royal Headpiece (page 37).

MAKE IT WEARABLE

16. Take the two long pieces of purple elastic that you prepared in step 14. Put the end of one of the elastic pieces through one of the front D-rings, and fold it 1½ inches (4 cm) over. Sew the folded elastic down, so it will stay connected to the D-ring. I used a sewing machine for this, but it can also be sewn by hand with a needle and thread. If you want to make the seam extra secure, you can optionally add some fabric glue between the folded elastic, but make sure to wait for it to dry before sewing. Repeat this for the other D-ring on the front of the breastplate.

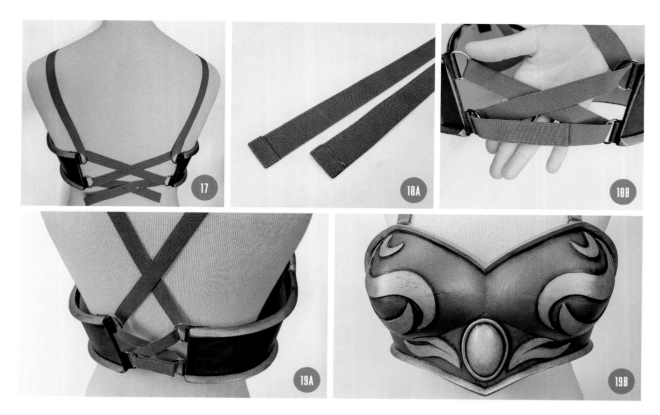

17. Put the breastplate on, and ask someone to help you for this step. Bring both elastics over the shoulders to the back and cross them. Loop them through the upper D-rings on the middle back of the breastplate and then cross them to the bottom D-rings on the breastplate so it resembles corset lacing. Then overlap the ends of the elastic in the middle. Check how tight you want it to fit, and mark a 2-inch (5-cm) overlap. Cut both elastic pieces to size. Take the breastplate off and pull the elastics out of the D-rings on the middle back, so you will have more room for the sewing machine in the next step.

18. Grab the 1½-inch (4-cm) Velcro. For both ends of elastic, fold the edge ½ inch (1 cm) over to prevent fraying. Then sew on the hook piece of the Velcro on one elastic and the loop piece on the other. Make sure to sew one end of the Velcro on the top of the elastic and the other on the bottom, so the attachment will work. While sewing the Velcro, you can immediately sew the folded edge of the elastic down so it stays flat. To make the seams extra secure, you can optionally add some fabric glue between the folded elastic and underneath the Velcro and wait for it to dry before sewing.

19. Now the attachments for the breastplate are done and you can wear the armor piece. It is recommended to ask someone to help you put it on because it can be hard to lace it by yourself.

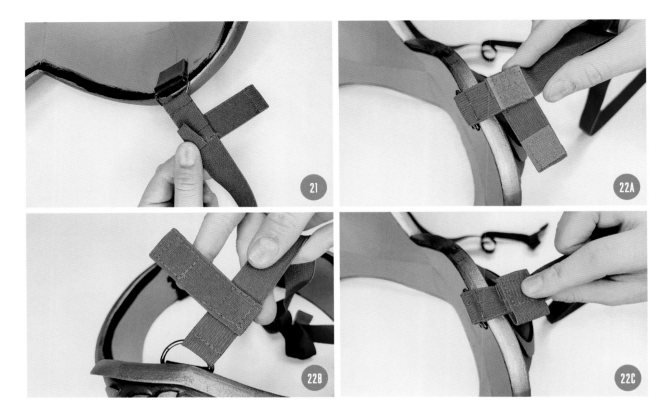

OPTIONAL: SHOULDER ARMOR ATTACHMENTS

Note: These steps are optional, but if you also created the Noble Layered Pauldrons (page 64) and want to wear these pieces together with this breastplate, you can create some extra attachments for them. The extra materials that you will need for this option are:

- **1 (7-inch [18-cm]) piece of ¾-inch (2-cm)-wide elastic (purple)**
- **1 (1½-inch [4-cm]) piece of ¾-inch (2-cm)-wide Velcro (purple)**

20. Cut the piece of elastic into two equal pieces. Also cut the Velcro into two equal pieces. You now have two pieces of 3½-inch (9-cm) purple elastic and two ¾-inch (2-cm) pieces of Velcro.

21. Take the breastplate strap on the front and put the piece of elastic on top of it, folding ½-inch (1-cm) around it. Optionally, use some fabric glue to keep this into place. Also fold ½-inch (1-cm) of the other edge of the elastic inside and secure with fabric glue.

22. Now flip it over so you can see the underside of the elastic. Put the hook part of the Velcro on one end of the elastic and secure it with fabric glue. Put the loop part of the Velcro on the other end of the elastic and secure it with fabric glue. Let the fabric glue dry for 10 minutes, and then sew over the two pieces of Velcro. Repeat these steps for the other strap.

Get Creative! Ideas for Variations

This project would also look really pretty in other color combinations. What about green and gold for a forest witch or red and orange for a fire wizard? You can adjust the detailing on the breastplate with your own designs to make it truly unique and fit with your character.

EVA foam prefabs, like the triangular bevels, can be pricey if you buy a lot of them. For a more cost-effective option, learn how to make your own on page 25.

You can add some faux fur to spice up the armor piece. Just cut a long strip of faux fur in a matching color, and with some hot glue, attach it to the inside edges of the breastplate.

23. The attachments for the pauldrons are now finished, and to wear the pauldrons with the breastplate, you can loop the elastic with Velcro through the D-ring on the front of the pauldron and close it so it is secured. On the back, you can just use the attachments that you already made on the pauldrons to keep them on your shoulders.

MATERIALS

Knight Chestplate templates (pattern sheets V and VI)

1 (22 x 18-inch [55 x 45-cm]) sheet of 6mm EVA foam

1 (4 x 4-inch [10 x 10-cm]) piece of 2mm EVA foam

6 feet (1.8-m) of ½-inch (1-cm)-wide 2mm EVA foam

2-inch (5-cm)-wide elastic (brown)

1 (9½-inch [24-cm]) piece of 2-inch (5-cm)-wide buckram ribbon

Contact cement

Filler (optional)

Flexible primer (black)

Acrylic paint (dark brown, silver and gold)

Oil paint (black) (optional)

Satin (spray) varnish (optional)

Fabric glue

Hot glue stick (optional)

1 (2-inch [5-cm]) piece of 1½-inch (4-cm)-wide Velcro

KNIGHT CHESTPLATE
Heavy-Plate Armor with Golden Decoration

This silver chest armor piece with golden lily decoration looks great on a knight or warrior costume. Wear it with a tunic or over a dress and add other armor pieces if you like. This chestplate looks really epic with the Battleworn Shoulder Armor and Gorget (page 72) worn on top of it. This piece can be used in costumes for many different character designs. The original shape of this chestplate is curvy, but it can be made more gender-neutral by flattening the curve a bit. The chestplate closes on the back with wide elastic straps, making it really comfortable to wear.

PREPARATION

If you want to make the chestplate more gender-neutral, follow the suggestion lines on the template to change the shape and make it less curvy. Otherwise use the template as is.

Since this piece doesn't close fully around the body, the template should fit most people. You can still decide to make it smaller or bigger of course. On the widest part (bustline), the chestplate measures a total width of 19½ inches (50 cm). Under the bust, it is 17½ inches (44 cm). The length in the middle from neckline to the bottom of the chestplate measures 10½ inches (27 cm).

Measure yourself to see if this will fit you. Keep in mind that the armor piece won't close in the back.

To make it bigger: Add more length to the edges on the sides and to the shoulder straps.

To make it longer: Add length to the bottom of both the base pattern pieces.

To make it wider: Add extra width to the middle front.

Cut the chestplate base pieces (middle, front and sides) and the lily decoration out of the 6mm EVA foam.

Cut the square of 2mm EVA foam into four (2 x 2-inch [5 x 5-cm]) squares.

To decide how much elastic you will need for the straps, take some more body measurements. Measure your underbust circumference (a bit above the waist) and subtract the width of the chestplate (17½ inches [44 cm]) from this measurement. That is the open room that you will have on your back between the two openings of the chestplate. Now add 7 inches (18 cm) to this measurement to make up for the overlap in the middle back and to attach the straps behind the chestplate. For me, that was 26 inches (66 cm). Cut that length out of the brown elastic, and then cut it in half. These are the two pieces needed for the back strap.

For the shoulder straps, measure from the top of your shoulder (between the shoulder tip and your neck, where a shoulder strap would be sitting) until the bottom of your shoulder blade (bra strap level). It can be hard to take this measurement by yourself, so ask someone to help you if possible.

Now add 5 inches (12 cm) to that measurement to make up for sewing it to the back strap and to attach it to the armor shoulder strap. For me, that was 17½ inches (45 cm). Cut that length out of the brown elastic twice.

You have four pieces of elastic: two for the back strap and two for the shoulder straps. If you want to be extra sure, you can always cut longer pieces of elastic and cut any excess off when you are actually making the attachments for the armor piece.

Cut the buckram ribbon into four equal pieces.

TOOLS

Paint marker

Craft knife

Measuring tape

Cutting mat

Heat gun

Safety tools, including a respirator, dust mask and safety glasses (review page 16)

Rotary tool with sanding drum (120-grit), or regular sandpaper

Brushes and sponges for painting

Sewing machine or needle and thread

Hot glue gun (optional)

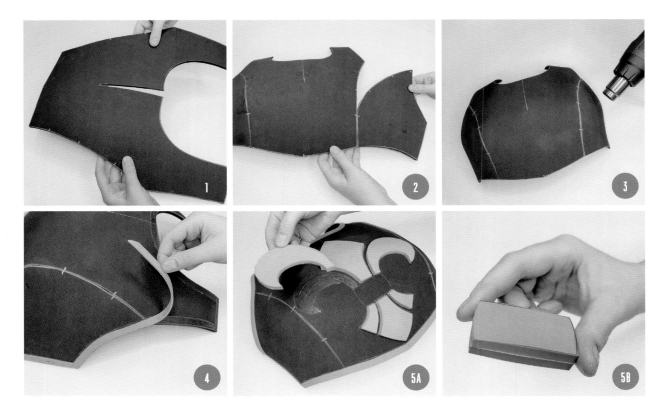

BUILDING THE BASE

1. Close the dart on the chestplate middle piece with the contact cement to shape the neckline.

2. Glue one of the side pieces to the middle piece. Use the registration marks as a guide for connecting the pieces. Then glue the other side piece to the middle and try to make it as symmetrical as possible.

SHAPING THE BASE

3. After the glue has fully set on the chestplate, heat the armor piece with the heat gun. When the foam is hot, you can shape it to be rounder and to fit better around your body. Hold the armor piece for a few minutes in the desired shape until it's cooled down so the foam will keep this shape. If you want to keep the chestplate simple, continue with step 6 now and skip the details.

DECORATING THE CHEST PIECE

4. Measure, cut and glue the ½-inch (1-cm)-wide strip of 2mm thick EVA foam along the edges of the chestplate. For neat corners, remember to cut the strips diagonally and to also apply glue where their edges meet. On the middle bottom of the chestplate, the corner is not super sharp, so you can follow that curve with a single piece of foam strip. You should end up with eight pieces of edging for the chestplate.

5. Glue the petals of the lily decoration to the chestplate using the contact cement. Stack and glue the two parts for the middle of the lily to get a thicker piece of foam, then set this piece aside.

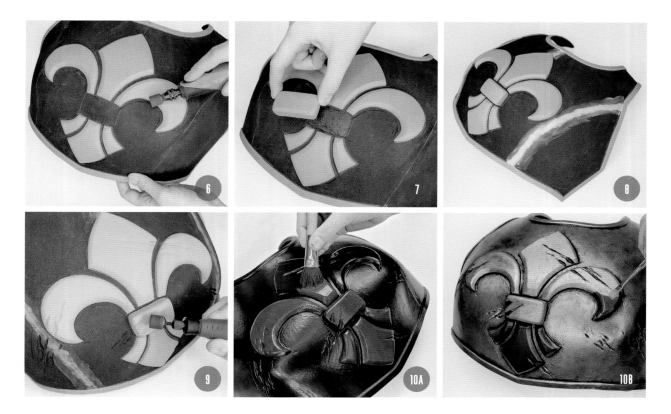

CLEANING UP THE EDGES

6. Use the rotary tool with a sanding drum attached to it (120-grit) to sand the edges of the chestplate. The transition between the glued-on edges and the armor piece will get super smooth in this step. Also sand the glue seams and the edges of the lily decoration. Sand the double-layered middle of the lily detail. Only sand the sides and the top, and leave the bottom flat.

The result of the sanding will look nicest when using a rotary tool, but you can also use regular sandpaper. After the sanding is done, clean the foam piece by removing all of the dust.

7. Glue the smoothed-out lily middle to the middle of the chestplate to finish the decoration.

OPTIONAL: SMOOTHING SEAMS WITH FILLER

8. If these seams are already smooth from the sanding, then skip this step. For smoothing the seams, apply some filler on the seams and smooth it out after adding some water to it. Leave the filler to dry overnight, and add more layers if necessary.

CREATING BATTLE DAMAGE

9. If you want to add battle damage to the chestplate, review the technique on page 24.

PRIMING AND PAINTING

10. Prime, paint and, optionally, protect the paint job with some varnish by using the same technique from steps 32 through 36 from the Battleworn Shoulder Armor and Gorget project (page 80).

MAKE IT WEARABLE: THE BACK STRAPS

11. Place one piece of elastic on the table with a piece of buckram ribbon on top of it, ½ inch (1 cm) from the edge. Fold that edge of elastic over the buckram ribbon to prevent fraying. Fold the opposite edge of the buckram ribbon to the inside, also to prevent fraying. Use some fabric glue to keep everything in place and leave the glue to dry for 10 minutes.

12. Place the 2 x 2-inch (5 x 5-cm) piece of 2-mm EVA foam on top of the buckram ribbon and elastic edge. Use some fabric glue to keep it in place and leave the glue to dry for 10 minutes. Then with a long, straight stitch on the sewing machine, sew the piece of foam onto the fabric. It's important that it's a long stitch and that you don't stitch too close to the edge of the foam, because we want as few holes in the foam as possible while still making a strong connection. With just a regular needle on the machine, and a non-stick sewing foot (or even better with a walking foot), this should work. If you don't have a sewing machine or don't want to try sewing foam with it, you can also do the stitching by hand with a sharp needle and some thread.

13. Apply a thin layer of contact cement to the EVA foam on the strap and on the inside of the side of the chestplate, then press the strap firmly to the inside of the armor piece. This connection will be strong because contact cement works amazing on EVA foam.

14. Optionally add some hot glue around the fabric on the EVA foam to make the connection even stronger. Repeat these steps for the second elastic back strap.

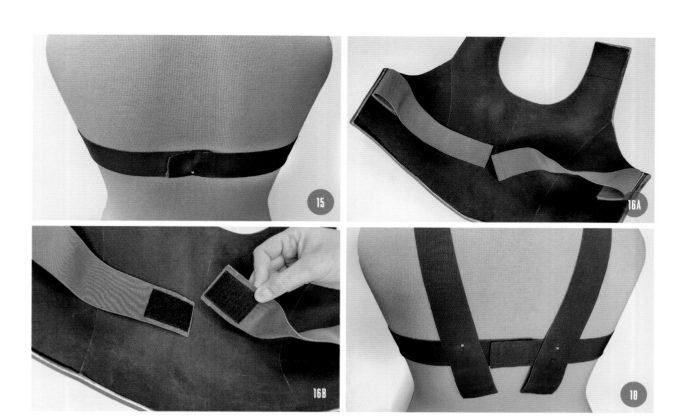

15. Try the chestplate on now that both back straps are attached to the sides. Overlap the ends of the elastic on your back. Ask someone to help you mark where the pieces overlap. Take the chestplate off and cut away excess elastic until the overlap is 2½ inches (6 cm) on each end of the elastic.

16. Place the hook part of the Velcro on the underside of one of the back strap's edges. Make sure that ½ inch (1 cm) of the elastic's edge is folded underneath the hook piece to prevent fraying of the elastic. Optionally add some fabric glue to secure it and leave the glue to dry for 10 minutes. Sew the hook piece onto the elastic with a sewing machine.

For the other back strap, sew the loop part of the Velcro on the top of the elastic. Also make sure to fold the edge of the elastic underneath the loop piece to prevent fraying. Optionally add some fabric glue to secure it and leave the glue to dry for 10 minutes. If you don't want to use a sewing machine or don't have one, do the sewing by hand with needle and thread. The back straps are now finished.

ATTACH THE SHOULDER STRAPS

17. Take the remaining two pieces of elastic for the shoulder straps, the two remaining buckram ribbon pieces and the two foam squares. Repeat steps 11 through 14 from this project to attach the buckram ribbon and foam squares on both ends of the pieces of elastic. In step 13 though, instead of gluing the straps to the sides of the chestplate, glue these to the ends of both the shoulder straps of the chestplate.

18. To determine how long the back straps need to be, try on the chestplate again. Ask someone to help you to hold the shoulder straps on your back, over the back strap. Mark where they meet the top edge of the back strap, and also the place on the back strap where they will be attached. Take the chestplate off.

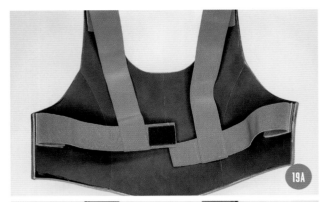

19. Put the shoulder straps on the back straps where they are marked. Cut off the excess length of elastic from the back straps. Fold ½ inch (1 cm) of the elastic's edge to the inside to prevent fraying. Use fabric glue to keep this in place and leave the glue to dry for 10 minutes. Then attach the shoulder strap to the back strap by sewing. Repeat this step for the other shoulder strap.

The attachments for the chestplate are finished, and you can wear it with your costume! Just put it on like a bra and close it on the back with the Velcro on the elastic band.

MATERIALS

Corset Belt templates (pattern sheets III and IV)

1 wide piece of 2mm EVA foam (I used a 30 x 5-inch [75 x 13-cm] piece)

1 piece of brown stretchy faux leather (I used a 31 x 6½-inch [79 x 16-cm] piece)

1 (7 x 5-inch [18 x 12-cm]) piece of 6mm EVA foam

Fabric glue

6 (4-mm-diameter) metal eyelets

Flexible primer (black)

Acrylic paint (dark brown)

Wax paint or metallic acrylic paint

Glossy (spray) varnish

Hot glue stick (optional)

1 (4-foot [120-cm]) length of cord

TOOLS

Paint marker

Measuring tape

Craft knife

Cutting mat

Sewing machine or needle and thread

Belt puncher or hole puncher

Eyelet pressing tool (optional)

Rotary tool with sanding drum (120-grit), or regular sandpaper

Safety tools, including a respirator, dust mask and safety glasses (review page 16)

Heat gun

Brushes and a piece of cloth for painting

Hot glue gun (optional)

CORSET BELT
With Elven Decoration

This corseted belt with elegant elvish markings looks amazing with the whole wood elf costume (page 6). It can be worn, combined with armor pieces, but it will also look great on just a dress or a tunic.

The EVA foam inside the belt gives it structure and strength, and the faux leather is actually sewn onto the foam. If you are worried that your sewing machine won't be able to sew through faux leather and foam, you can also do the stitching by hand or just use glue. The belt can be made more gender-neutral by making it less pointy on the front and/or by making it wider. The elvish detail on the front of the belt is painted with gilding wax to make it look beautifully antique.

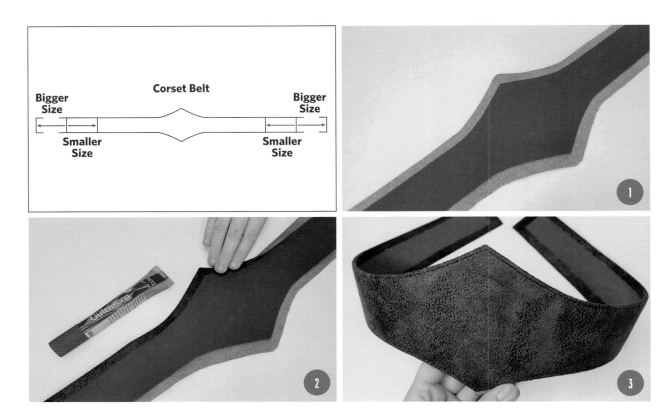

PREPARATION

Determine if the original template will fit you. Measure and write down your waist circumference. The original template will result in a belt that would fit a minimum of a 31½-inch (80-cm) waist, where the belt will have a 2 inch (5 cm) gap for lacing in the back. Otherwise, if you want to make a lace-up closure, take off 2 inches (5 cm) from your waist measurement. If you want to fully close the belt, then make the belt as long as your waist circumference is. After you've measured your waist, add or take away length from the template of the belt on both sides so it will fit around your waist.

Cut the whole belt shape out of the 2mm EVA foam. Use your foam belt as a template to cut the piece of faux leather (preferably with some stretch in it), and add ½ inch (1 cm) of folding allowance around the edges. On the two ends of the belt, add close to 1 inch (2.5 cm) of allowance. This will make the part where the eyelets will be attached stronger. If your faux leather isn't stretchy, make some cuts in the allowance to allow it to fold over the curved shape of the foam. If the faux leather is stretchy enough, it's possible that this isn't needed.

Cut the elven knotwork decoration out of the 6mm EVA foam. Use a sharp knife to cut all the fine details.

CREATE THE BASE OF THE BELT

1. Use the fabric glue to glue the foam belt onto the faux leather. Place it right in the middle so there's enough faux leather left around all the edges.

2. Apply fabric glue to the folding allowance on the inside of the faux leather and fold it over the edge of the craft foam belt. Press it down tightly until the glue dries and it stays in place.

3. With your sewing machine, top stitch with a rather long straight stitch around the whole belt, ⅛ inch (3 mm) from the edge. With just a regular needle on the machine, and a nonstick sewing foot (or even better, with a walking foot), this should work. If you don't have a sewing machine, or don't want to try sewing foam with it, you can also do the stitching by hand with a sharp needle and thread.

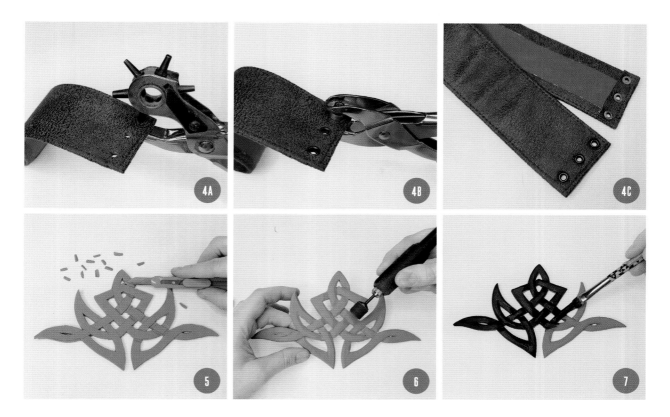

ADDING THE EYELETS

4. You'll use three eyelets for each end of the belt. Mark where you want them and punch the holes for the eyelets with the belt puncher or hole puncher.

Insert the eyelets. It's easiest with an eyelet pressing tool. If you don't have an eyelet pressing tool, you can use the little tools that usually come with a pack of eyelets, and press the eyelets into the belt with a hammer.

The base of the belt is now finished! If you don't want a decoration on it, you're now done with this project. Simply lace up the belt with the cord and you are ready to go! However, don't lace it too tightly, because in the end, the material is still foam, and you don't want it to rip.

SHAPING THE ELVISH DECORATION

5. With a sharp knife, cut away pieces of the elvish decoration as indicated. This doesn't need to be super exact because you'll be sanding it smooth in the next step.

6. Using the rotary tool with 120-grit sanding drum, sand the edges of the knotwork smooth. Also sand the parts you carved out in step 5. The result of the sanding will look nicest when using a rotary tool, but you can also use regular sandpaper. After the sanding is done, clean the foam piece by removing all of the dust and heat-seal it with the heat gun.

PRIMING AND PAINTING THE DECORATION

7. Apply a flexible primer onto the knotwork. Use as many coats of primer as needed until you like how the surface looks. I used two layers of HexFlex black. Allow it to dry for 2 to 4 hours.

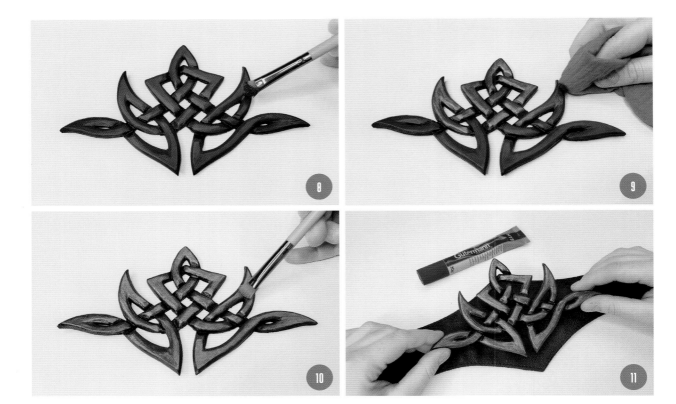

8. Apply a layer of brown acrylic paint on the raised parts of the knotwork. Leave the parts that need shadows black. This already gives it some depth. If your primer wasn't black, then you can also add some black paint on the shadow parts. Leave the brown paint to dry for 2 to 4 hours.

9. To get a beautiful golden color on the piece, apply the gilding wax to the foam with an old piece of cloth (I used Rub 'n Buff Grecian Gold). Only paint the raised surface, and not the shadows. The gilding wax doesn't need much time to dry, so you can continue immediately with the next step. If you can't find gilding wax, you can use metallic acrylic paint instead.

10. To protect the paint job, paint or spray the whole piece with a glossy acrylic varnish. In this example I used a brush-on acrylic varnish. The glossy varnish also helps with making the elvish decoration look more like real shiny metal. Let the piece dry overnight.

ADDING THE DECORATION TO THE BELT

11. Use fabric glue, hot glue or super glue to glue the knotwork to the middle front of the belt. The corseted belt is finished, and you can wear it with your outfit by lacing it up with the cord through the eyelets on the back.

Get Creative! Ideas for Variations

You can design your own decoration if you don't want to use the elvish knotwork. For example, a crescent moon or runes can look really beautiful. By using a different color of faux leather or even one with a special texture on it, you can create a belt that will perfectly complement your outfit.

If you don't like the lacing, you can also lengthen the belt and add a buckle. Or make the belt long enough so it overlaps just a bit and sew some Velcro on both ends to close it.

MATERIALS

Regal Hip Armor templates (digital pattern plus pattern sheet V)

1 (24 x 14-inch [60 x 35-cm]) sheet of 6mm EVA foam

1 (14 x 10-inch [35 x 25-cm]) piece of 2mm EVA foam

1 (¾-inch [2-cm])-wide piece of elastic (purple)

Contact cement

7½ feet (2.3 m) of EVA foam prefab triangular bevel (I used 10mm wide, high profile)

7 inches (18 cm) of EVA foam prefab half-round dowel (I used 5mm wide)

Foam clay

Filler (optional)

Flexible primer (black)

Acrylic paint (dark brown, metallic purple, pearl, gold and silver)

Oil paint (black) (optional)

Satin and glossy (spray) varnish (optional)

1 (2-inch [5-cm]) piece of 1½-inch (4-cm)-wide Velcro (purple)

Fabric glue (optional)

(continued)

REGAL HIP ARMOR
With Shining Gemstones

The curvy shape of the hip plates accentuates a dramatic silhouette for any costume that they're worn with. These elegant armor pieces look amazing with a sorceress costume. They can be worn over a long, flowy skirt and won't restrict movement since the large pieces are on the sides and not on the front. The middle piece of the hip armor is like a decorative belt buckle and on top of it, a magnificent gem is shining. Painted with pearlescent paint and finished with glossy varnish, the gem made with foam clay is a stunning centerpiece.

Paint marker

Craft knife

Cutting mat

Measuring tape

Heat gun

Safety tools, including a respirator, dust mask and safety glasses (review page 16)

Rotary tool with sanding drum (120-grit), or regular sandpaper

Wooden clay modeling tool (optional)

Brushes and sponges for painting

Sewing machine or needle and thread

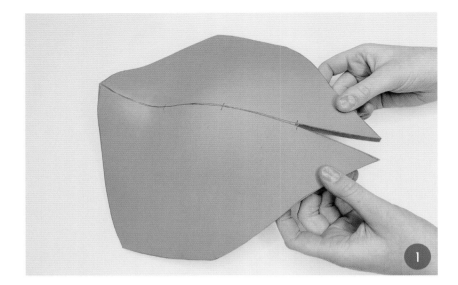

PREPARATION

Cut the hip plate base four times out of the 6mm EVA foam (twice mirrored). Cut the belt buckle out of the 6mm EVA foam too.

From the 2mm EVA foam, cut out the swirly details for the hip plates four times (twice mirrored) and the swirly details for the belt buckle twice (once mirrored). You will have fourteen detail pieces in the end.

Cut eight (2½ x 1½-inch [6 x 4-cm]) strips of 2mm EVA foam. These will be used to attach the armor pieces to an elastic belt.

To determine how much elastic you will need, take some measurements. Measure your hips (at the height where you want to wear the armor), and add 2 inches (5 cm) to this measurement to allow for some overlap on the back. For the example, I cut the purple elastic to 45 inches (115 cm).

BUILDING THE BASE PIECES

1. Glue both middle edges of the hip plate pieces together. Use the registration marks as a guide for connecting the pieces. Repeat for the other hip plate.

SHAPING THE ARMOR PIECES

2. After the glue has fully set, heat the armor piece with the heat gun. When the foam is hot, you can shape it to be rounded and fit on your hips. Be careful that the foam is not too hot when you shape it over your body. When you like the round shape, also curl up the bottom tip and the top tip to create an interesting silhouette. Hold the armor piece for a few minutes in the desired shape until it's cooled down, so the foam will stay in this shape. Repeat these steps for the other hip plate.

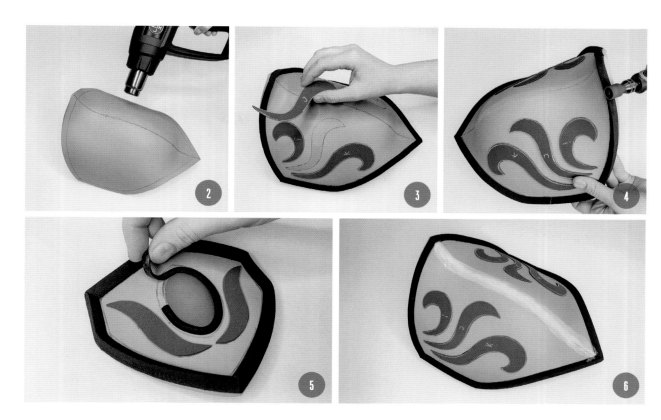

Also heat-shape the belt buckle piece so it is a bit rounded. That will make it fit better to the front of the body. If you want to keep the project simple and leave the details out, skip steps 3 and 5.

DECORATING THE ARMOR

3. Measure, cut and glue the triangular-shaped bevel along the edges of the hip plates and belt buckle. You should end up with eleven pieces of bevel to decorate the edges. Also glue on the fourteen swirly details.

CLEANING UP THE EDGES

4. Using the rotary tool with 120-grit sanding drum, sand the edges of the armor pieces smooth. Also sand the glue seams on the hip plates. The result of the sanding will look nicest when using a rotary tool, but you can also use regular sandpaper. After the sanding is done, remove all of the dust.

CREATING A FAUX GEMSTONE

5. To create a faux gemstone with foam clay for the middle of the belt buckle, follow steps 6 and 7 from the Royal Head-piece (page 39).

OPTIONAL: SMOOTHING SEAMS WITH FILLER

6. This step is optional and you can do this to hide the glue seams on the hip plates even more. If these seams are already nicely smooth from the sanding, simply skip this step. For smoothing the seams, apply some filler on the seams and smooth it out after adding some water to it (page 23). Leave the filler to dry overnight, and add more layers if necessary.

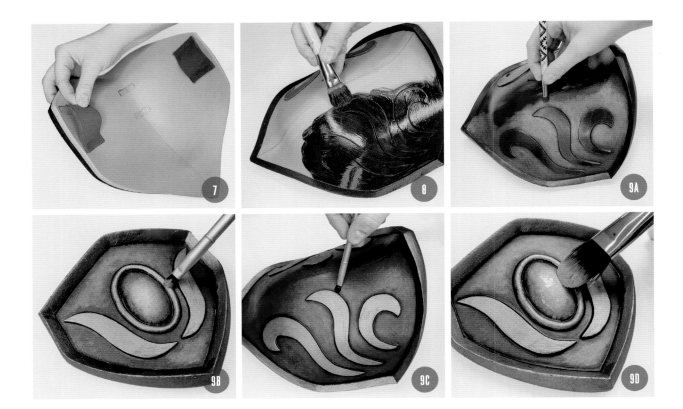

ADDING LOOPS FOR THE BELT

7. Turn the armor pieces upside down on the table. Take the little strips of the 2mm EVA foam and put them on the back of the armor pieces to decide where they need to go. Two go on the back of the belt buckle, one on each side. Three go on each hip plate, one on each side and one in the middle. Mark the top of these strips on the armor piece. On the bottom of the strips, mark the line ¼ inch (0.5-cm) higher. Apply a thin, ½-inch (1-cm)-wide layer of contact cement between both of those lines, and on the top and bottom of the foam strips. Make sure that there is no glue in the middle of the strips, since this is where the elastic belt will be pulled through in the end to make the armor pieces wearable. When the glue is tacky, place the foam strips on the armor pieces. Make sure that the foam strip will be curved, so there is an opening for the belt. Repeat this for the belt buckle and the other plate.

PRIMING AND PAINTING

8. Prepare the pieces for priming and painting by heat-sealing them. Try to avoid the foam clay on the buckle, because that can be damaged by the heat. When the foam is cool, apply a flexible primer onto the armor pieces. Cover the complete outside of the pieces and also a bit on the inside (about 1 inch [2.5 cm]). The curved part at the top of the hip plates will be visible from the underside, so be sure to cover that in primer too. I used two layers of HexFlex black. Leave the primer to dry for two to four hours.

9. To paint the hip armor and finish the paint job, use the technique that's described in steps 10 through 15 of the Royal Headpiece (pages 40 and 41).

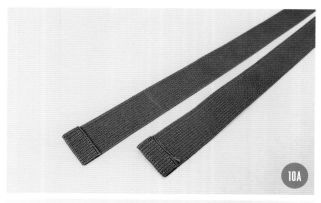

MAKE IT WEARABLE

10. Fold over the last ½ inch (1 cm) of both the ends of the elastic and sew the Velcro on top of those ends. You can optionally put some fabric glue underneath the fold and the Velcro before sewing to make the connection stronger.

Sew the hook part to one end of the elastic and the loop part to the other end. Make sure that one is sewn on the top, and the other on the bottom of the elastic, so the Velcro will function without having to twist the elastic. I used a sewing machine to sew this down, but you can sew it by hand too.

11. Pull the elastic belt through the loops on the back of the pieces and close the Velcro in the back. To wear the armor, simply open the belt, put it over your hips and close it on the back.

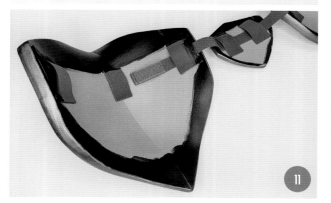

Get Creative! Ideas for Variations

If you don't like the pointy shape of the hip plates, you can adjust the template to make the edges more rounded. The plates in this example are only one layer, but you can add more layers to change the silhouette.

You can easily personalize this project by changing the designs of the decorations and the color of the armor. My sorceress has purple armor with golden details, but this would also look epic in dark red with bronze details.

In my version, the belt is made with purple elastic, but it can be a sewn faux leather belt too. By adding strips of fabric hanging down from the belt, you can create an extra layer for your costume. While walking about, those strips will move in the wind, giving cool effects for photoshoots.

LEGAND FOOT ARMOR

MATERIALS

Layered Elven Greaves templates (digital pattern)

1 (32 x 28-inch [80 x 70-cm]) sheet of 6mm EVA foam

1 (8 x 6-inch [20 x 15-cm]) piece of 2mm EVA foam

1 (1¾-inch [4.5-cm])-wide strip of faux leather (green or brown)

Contact cement

4 feet (1.2-m) of EVA foam prefab half-round dowel (I used 5mm wide)

Foam clay

Flexible primer (black)

Acrylic paint (dark brown and light brown)

Wax paint (I used Rub 'n Buff gold) or metallic acrylic paint

Matte and glossy (spray) varnish (optional)

6 metal buckles (mine were 1 inch [2.5 cm] wide)

24 brass fasteners (mine were ¾ inch [2 cm] long in gold)

(continued)

LAYERED ELVEN GREAVES
With Golden Leaves

These leg armor pieces are built by stacking multiple layers of foam, resulting in an interesting shape with pointy edges. They close with multiple faux leather straps and buckles, so they are adjustable and can be worn over various kinds of leg and footwear. Wear these beautiful greaves over boots, or wear cozy and warm (faux fur) leg warmers underneath. Because the base of these greaves is painted brown instead of metallic, they look like they're made out of thick leather, which fits perfectly with a wood elf character. The leaf details are sculpted with foam clay, so you can add as many or as little of these as you want.

TOOLS

Paint marker

Craft knife

Cutting mat

Measuring tape

Heat gun

Safety tools, including a respirator, dust mask and safety glasses (review page 16)

Rotary tool with sanding drum (120-grit), or regular sandpaper

Wooden clay modeling tool

Brushes and a piece of cloth for painting

Sewing machine or needle and thread (optional)

Belt puncher or hole puncher

PREPARATION

The greaves don't close completely around the legs, so you shouldn't need to resize the template. Use your template to trace and cut all the pattern pieces for the greaves four times out of the 6mm EVA foam (twice mirrored). Make sure to cut the foam at an inward angle.

With the 2mm EVA foam, cut six (2 x 2-inch [5 x 5-cm]) strips and twelve (2 x 1-inch [5 x 2.5-cm]) strips. These will be used at the end of the process to help keep the straps on the armor pieces.

Take some measurements to determine how long your strip of faux leather will need to be for the straps. Choose what leg and footwear you want to wear underneath the greaves, and then measure around your ankles, the middle of the calf and just below the knees. Add 6 inches (15 cm) to each of those measurements to allow room for the buckles. Write these measurements down and cut strips of those lengths. You need two of each length, one for each greave. I ended up needing a total of 61 inches (155 cm) of faux leather.

The width of the strips depends on the buckle size. I used 1-inch (2.5-cm)-wide buckles, so the straps need to be that width too. With a ½-inch (1-cm) seam allowance on the edges, I needed to cut strips that were 1¾ inch (4.5 cm) wide. If you can find faux leather that is a bit stretchy, it will help with making these armor pieces more comfortable.

BUILDING THE LAYERS

1. Take the left and right piece for the first layer and apply a thin layer of contact cement to both the middle edges. When the glue is tacky, connect the two pieces to form one layer for the greaves. Repeat this for all the other layers.

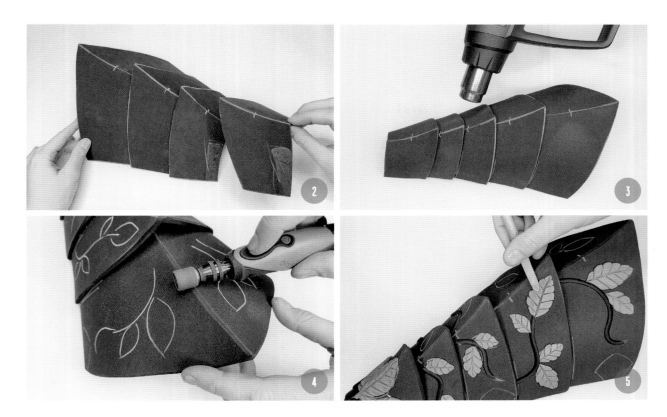

2. Stack the five layers for each greave and see how they fit on your legs. Decide where you want the layers to be attached to each other and mark this with a paint marker so you know where to apply the contact cement. Now, apply a thin layer of glue to the underside of the top layer and the outside of the under layer. Only apply the glue on the sides, and not over the whole layer (see image). When the glue is tacky, press the layers on top of each other. Repeat this until the full leg armor piece is formed. Repeat for the other leg.

HEAT-SHAPING

3. Heat the leg armor with the heat gun. When the foam is hot, you can shape it so it is more curved and fits nicely over your leg. Be careful that the foam is not too hot, since you will be shaping it on your leg. When the armor piece is in the desired shape, hold it for a few minutes until it cools so it stays in its new shape. Repeat for the other leg.

OPTIONAL: CLEANING UP THE EDGES

4. If you already like how the edges of the foam look, skip this step.

Otherwise, using the rotary tool with 120-grit sanding drum, sand the edges of the armor pieces smooth. The result of the sanding will look nicest when using a rotary tool, but you can also use sandpaper for this job. After the sanding is done, clean the foam piece by removing all of the dust. If you don't want to add the leaf details, skip step 5.

ADD STEMS AND FOAM CLAY LEAVES

5. Decide where you want the stems for the decorative leaves to go and mark them with a paint marker on the foam. To add stems and foam clay leaves, follow steps 9 through 12 of the Layered Elven Bracers (pages 86 and 87).

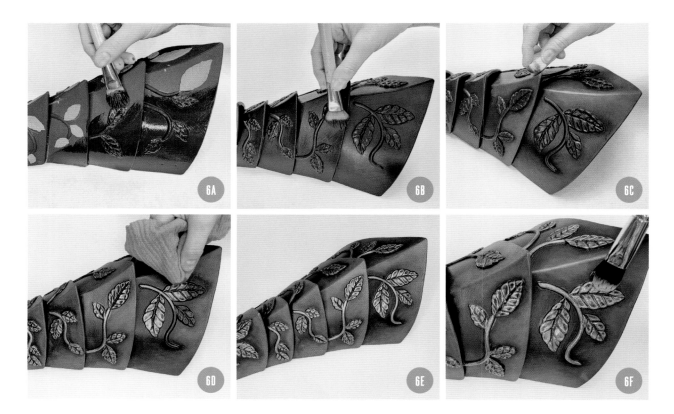

PRIMING AND PAINTING

6. To paint the greaves and finish the paint job, use the same technique that's described in steps 13 through 18 of the Layered Elven Bracers (pages 87 and 88).

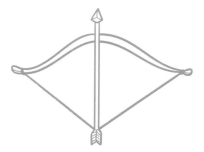

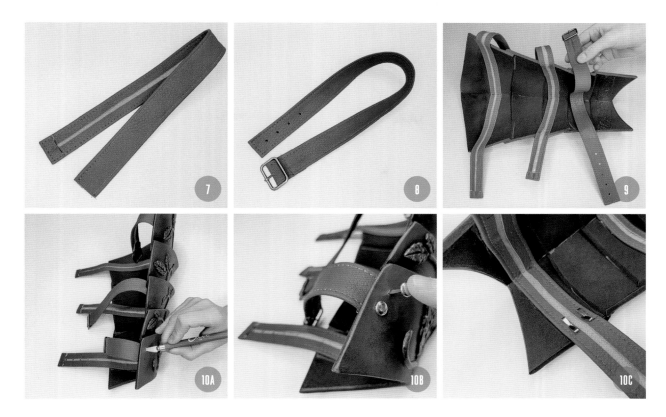

MAKE THEM WEARABLE

7. Hem the edges of the six pleather strips by topstitching with the sewing machine. If you don't have a sewing machine, you can leave the straps unhemmed or sew by hand with needle and thread.

8. Attach a buckle to one end of each strap. To do this, loop one end of the strap through the buckle and mark where the pin of the buckle should go. Then take the strap out of the buckle and punch a hole for the pin, using the belt puncher or hole puncher. Now pull the strap through the buckle and put the pin through the hole. Fold the strap back and sew it closed so the buckle is attached. You can add some fabric glue before sewing to make the connection stronger. On the other end of the strap, punch some holes with a belt puncher or hole puncher.

9. Flip the armor piece so it's upside down and lay three straps on it to see where you want to place them. Mark where the straps will go, and then add some contact cement to both the inside of the armor and the outside of the strap where it needs to be attached. When the glue is tacky, push the straps firmly to the inside of the armor. Repeat this for the other greave.

10. For each strap, you'll need four brass fasteners. On the outside of the armor, poke them through the foam. You'll probably need to cut a tiny slit inside of the pleather with the craft knife to make the fastener go through. Then fold the ends of the fastener open on the inside of the foam. Add another fastener to the same strap. If the ends of the fasteners are too long, fold them in half. Repeat this for the other straps.

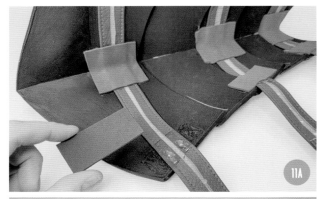

11. Each leg armor piece will need three of the 2 x 2-inch (5 x 5-cm) squares and six of the 2 x 1-inch (5 x 2.5-cm) strips. Glue the thin strips to the inside of the foam, over the spots where the brass fasteners are. Glue the squares to the inside of the foam, over the straps, in the middle of the armor. These extra pieces of foam will help to secure the straps in place.

The layered greaves can now be worn by putting them on your legs, and then closing the buckles.

GALLANT HEAVY LEG ARMOR

With Knee Guards

These leg armor pieces wrap fully around the lower leg, making them look super epic. This "heavy" armor is really not heavy at all because it's completely made out of lightweight EVA foam! Isn't cosplay just magic? This leg armor is perfect for a knight in shining armor. Attached to the front part are kneecaps that make the shape of these armor pieces extra interesting. Held together with elastic straps, these pieces will stay securely on your legs. I recommend wearing this armor over a pair of leggings or trousers to make it more comfortable.

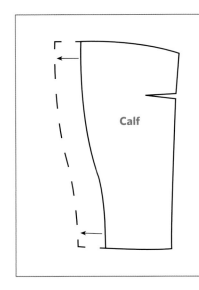

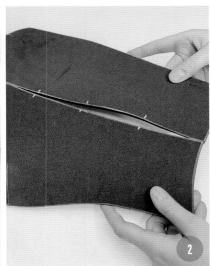

PREPARATION

Before cutting the foam, take some measurements to determine if you need to adjust the template and see how much elastic you will need for the attachments. Wear the shoes and legwear that you want to wear underneath this armor and measure around your ankles and 2 inches (5 cm) below your knee. Add 3 inches (8 cm) to both measurements and cut the pieces of elastic in those measurements. You will need four pieces of elastic—two for each leg. I needed a total of 67 inches (170 cm) of elastic.

Use these measurements to check if the original template will fit you. The maximum width of the top (calf) is 21½ inches (55 cm), and the maximum width of the bottom (ankle) is 14½ inches (37 cm). If that is too small, add some extra width to the calf pattern piece to make the leg armor wider (see image).

Cut all the pattern pieces for the front of the leg armor twice out of the 6mm EVA foam (once mirrored). Make sure to cut the front of the kneecap pieces at an inward angle and the bottom of the kneecap pieces (where they connect to the shin pieces) at an outward angle.

Cut the pieces for the back of the leg armor four times out of the 6mm EVA foam (twice mirrored).

Also cut the pieces for the lily decoration and the little circles for decoration out of the 6mm EVA foam.

Cut four (2 x 2-inch [5 x 5-cm]) strips and eight (2 x 1-inch [5 x 2.5-cm]) strips out of the 2mm EVA foam. These will be used to help keep the straps on the armor. Cut two (6 x 2-inch [15 x 5-cm]) rectangles out of the 2mm EVA foam. These will be used to attach the front and back of this armor together.

BUILDING THE SHIN PIECES

1. Close the dart on the outer shin piece with the contact cement. This dart will help give the armor a rounded shape on the side, so it fits nicely on the leg.

2. Glue the outer and inner shin pieces together. Use the registration marks as a guide for connecting the pieces.

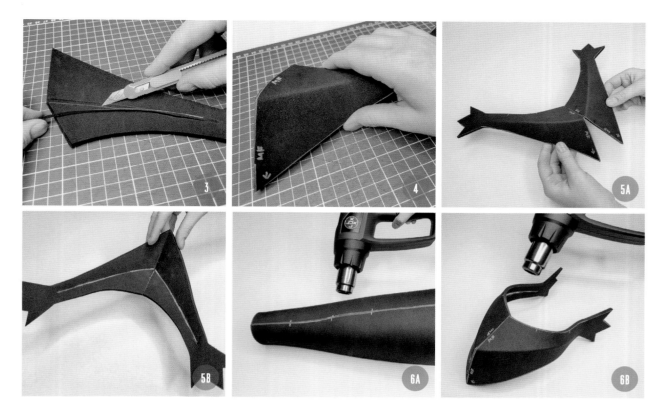

3. Flip the two kneecap halves upside down on the cutting mat. Mark the lines for the undercuts that are shown on the template. With a sharp craft knife, make V-shaped cuts on those lines. Make sure not to cut all the way through the foam.

4. Add some contact cement inside the grooves. When the glue is tacky, fold the grooves closed. This creates nice ridges on the other side (the top) of the foam.

5. Glue the inner and outer kneecap half together.

6. Heat the shin and the kneecap pieces with the heat gun. When the foam is hot, you can shape a rounder fit over your leg. Be careful that the foam is not too hot, since you will be shaping it on your leg. When the armor piece is in the desired shape, hold it for a few minutes until it is cooled down so it keeps its new shape.

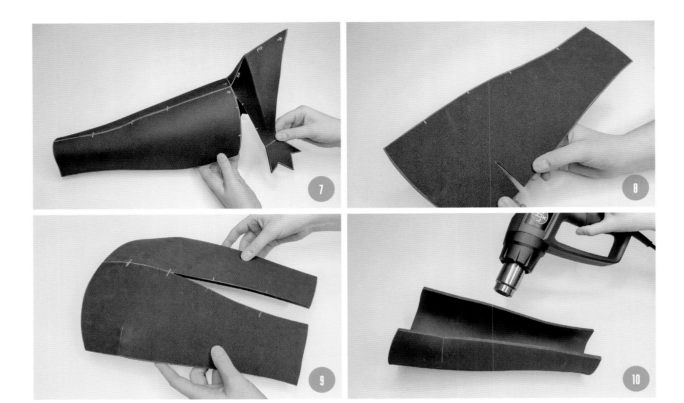

7. Glue the kneecap to the top edge of the shin piece, using the contact cement. Repeat steps 1 through 7 for the other leg.

BUILDING THE CALF PIECE

8. Close the darts on both of the calf piece halves with the contact cement.

9. Glue both calf halves together along the middle back edge, using the contact cement. Use the registration marks as a guide for connecting the pieces. Repeat these steps for the other leg.

10. Heat the calf pieces with the heat gun. When the foam is hot, you can shape them similar to how you did in step 6.

If you want to keep it simple, you can skip steps 11 through 14 and 16 and leave the detailing out.

DECORATING THE EDGES

11. Measure the ½-inch (1-cm)-wide strip of 2mm EVA foam around the edges of the armor pieces, and cut it to the right lengths. In order to achieve nice pointy corners, make sure to cut the ends diagonally.

For the shin piece, you will need an extra strip for the part where the kneecap is connected to the shin. That's six pieces per shin.

For the calf piece, cut strips only for the top and bottom edges (skip the sides). You will need two pieces of edging for the calf piece.

Note: You should end up with sixteen pieces of edging. In order not to mix these bevel pieces up, write numbers or letters on them and also on the corresponding part of the armor where they need to go.

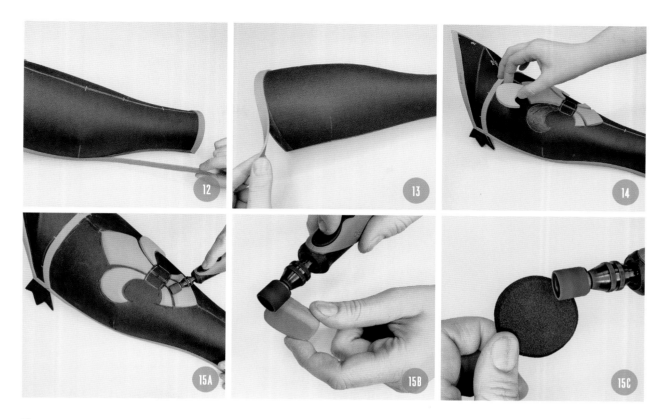

12. Glue the strips of foam to the shin piece all around the edge and where the two ends of the foam strip meet to form one continuous bevel. Also glue a strip of foam on the part where the kneecap connects to the shin.

13. On the calf piece, glue the strips of foam to both the top and the bottom edges. Repeat these steps for the other leg.

ADDING DETAILS

14. Take the petals of the lily decoration and glue them to the shin piece. Repeat this on the other shin piece and try to make it as symmetrical as possible. Leave the two pieces for the middle of the lily set aside for now, but glue the two middle pieces on top of each other to get a double-thick piece of foam.

CLEANING UP THE EDGES

15. Using the rotary tool with 120-grit sanding drum, sand the edges of the calf and shin pieces, the glue seams and the edges of the lily decoration. Sand the sides and top of the double-layered middle of the lily detail, leaving the bottom flat. Sand the edges of the 6mm foam circles. The result of the sanding will look nicest when using a rotary tool, but you can also use regular sandpaper. After the sanding is done, clean the foam piece by removing all of the dust.

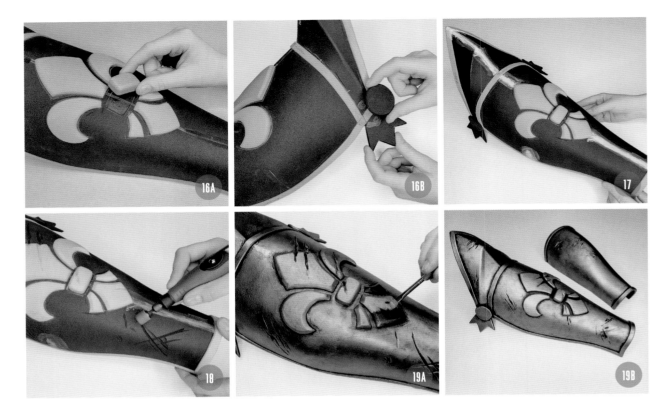

16. Glue the smoothed-out lily middle to the shin pieces to finish that part of the decoration.

Glue the circles to both sides of the kneecaps. There are two circles for each leg.

OPTIONAL: SMOOTHING SEAMS WITH FILLER

17. If the seams are already smooth from the sanding, simply skip this step. For smoothing the seams, apply some filler on the seams and smooth it out after adding some water to it (page 23). Leave the filler to dry overnight, and add more layers if necessary.

CREATING BATTLE DAMAGE

18. If you want to add battle damage, review the technique on page 24.

PRIMING AND PAINTING

19. Prime, paint and, optionally, protect the paint job with some varnish, using the same technique from steps 32 through 36 from the Battleworn Shoulder Armor and Gorget (page 80).

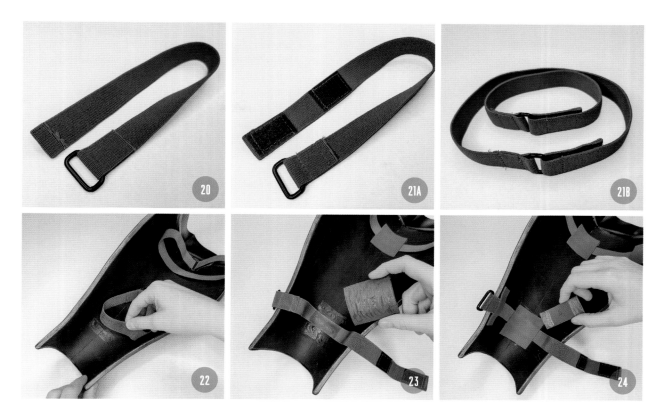

MAKE IT WEARABLE

20. Take one of the pieces of brown elastic and one of the metal rectangle rings. Put one end of the elastic through the metal ring and fold it over 1 inch (2.5 cm). Sew through the folded elastic to secure the metal ring to it. I used a sewing machine to sew this down, but you can sew it by hand too. Use some fabric glue to make this bond extra secure if you want.

21. Fold ½ inch (1 cm) of the other end of the elastic over to prevent fraying, and sew both sides of the Velcro to the elastic, leaving 1 inch (2.5 cm) free between them. You can optionally put some fabric glue underneath the fold and the Velcro before sewing to make the connection stronger.

Now you will have an elastic band that you can open and close with the Velcro and the metal ring. Repeat this for the other three pieces of elastic.

22. Place the shin armor piece upside down on the table. Place the larger elastic band on the top (under the knee) and the smaller band on the bottom (at the ankle) of the inside of the armor piece. Mark the height where you want to place these bands with a paint marker. In the middle, glue 2 inches (5 cm) of the elastic bands to the inside of the armor piece. Repeat this for the rest of the elastic bands.

23. The glue alone won't be strong enough to keep the elastic bands in place, so we will add some foam on top. Glue the 2 x 2-inch (5 x 5-cm) squares of 2mm EVA foam on top of the elastic bands and the armor pieces.

24. Glue the 2 x 1-inch (5 x 2.5-cm) strips of 2mm EVA foam over the elastic bands on the edge of the armor. Make sure to only apply glue on the part of the foam that will be touching the foam, and leave the elastic free of glue. This way, the elastic can still move back and forth underneath the foam strip. Add a foam strip to all eight sides of the elastic bands. The elastic straps are now fully attached.

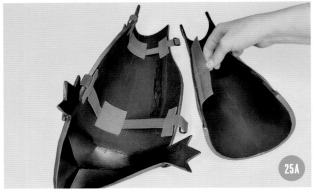

25A

25B

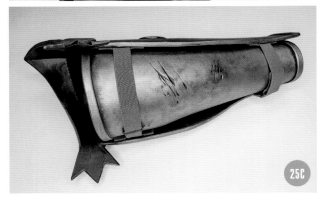

25C

25. Try the armor on your leg by first holding the calf part on your calf, and then holding the shin part on to your shin, covering the calf piece on the sides. Put the two elastic bands around the calf piece and close them with the Velcro. Now mark with some chalk on the armor where the armor overlaps on the outside of your leg and take the armor off. (Use chalk for the markings because it needs to be temporary.) On the inside of the armor, also mark where it overlaps. Now take one 6 x 2-inch (15 x 5-cm) rectangle of 2mm EVA foam and glue this to the inside of the armor, connecting the front and back piece together. This extra piece of foam will help to keep both parts in the correct place. Repeat this for the other leg.

The heavy leg armor pieces are now ready and you can wear them with your outfit! To put them on, first make sure the elastic bands are loose. Then put the armor piece on your leg and fasten the two elastic bands.

Note: Because the armor is open on one side, and the bands covering it are elastic, the armor can flex a bit while you move around. Since leg armor can be very uncomfortable, I always like to find a way to make it somewhat flexible.

Get Creative! Ideas for Variations

If you don't like the idea of having armor covering both the front and back of your leg, leave the back part off. You can still use the elastic bands for the attachments or glue some D-rings onto the sides of the armor and lace it up with elastic.

The kneecap part can be left out if you only want the armor to cover your lower leg, and not the knees.

There are many other options for textures other than metal. For example, add EVA foam scales on the armor to give it a texture like it is made out of dragon skin. Or leave out the decorative edges and paint the armor pieces brown to make them look like leather armor.

MATERIALS

Silver Foot Armor templates (digital pattern)

1 (¾-inch [2-cm]-wide) piece of elastic (in the color of your footwear)

1 (2½-inch [6-cm]) piece of ¾-inch (2-cm)-wide Velcro

1 (20 x 14–inch [50 x 35–cm]) sheet of 6mm EVA foam

1 (4 x 2–inch [10 x 5–cm]) piece of 2mm EVA foam

Contact cement

90 inches (2.3 m) of ½-inch (1-cm)-wide 2mm EVA foam

Filler (optional)

4 metal D-rings (I used 1-inch [2.5-cm]-wide D-rings)

Flexible primer (black)

Acrylic paint (silver)

Satin (spray) varnish (optional)

Fabric glue (optional)

TOOLS

Paint marker

Craft knife

Cutting mat

Heat gun

Safety tools, including a respirator, dust mask and safety glasses (review page 16)

Rotary tool with sanding drum (120-grit), or regular sandpaper

Brushes and sponges for painting

Sewing machine or needle and thread

SILVER FOOT ARMOR
With Elastic Attachments

These foot armor pieces are built up of two layers, and they sit on the instep of the foot and over the toes, also covering the bottom edge of leg armor (if you are wearing that). Elastic straps in the color of the footwear underneath keep these armor pieces right where they need to be. I wear them on high heel booties, but they fit on flats too. My version is made for a medieval knight look, but these are such a versatile shape that they will work with many different character designs and armor styles.

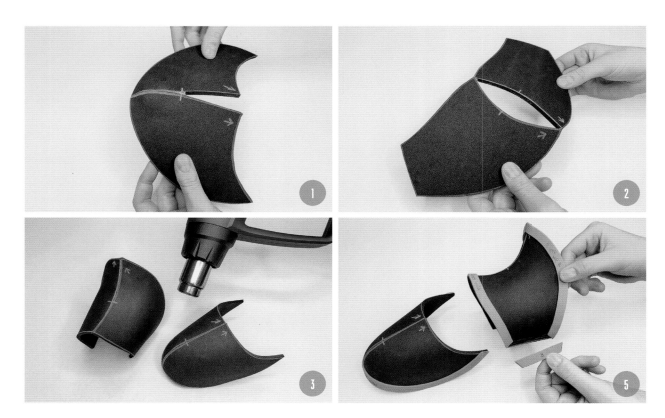

PREPARATION

For the attachments, I suggest starting with 1 yard (1 meter) of elastic in the color of the shoes that you plan to wear.

Cut the Velcro in half. Use the templates to trace and cut the foot armor base pieces four times out of the 6mm EVA foam (twice mirrored). Use the rectangle of 2mm EVA foam to cut four (2 x 1–inch [5 x 2.5–cm]) pieces. These will be used to attach the D-rings to the foam.

BUILDING THE BASES

1. Apply a thin layer of contact cement on both inside edges of the toe piece. When the glue is tacky, connect both halves of the toes together. Use the registration marks as a guide for connecting the pieces, to help make the armor piece as symmetrical as possible.

2. Glue both halves of the instep piece together along the top edge. Use the registration marks as a guide for connecting the pieces.

3. Heat the foam with the heat gun. When the foam is hot, you can shape it to be more rounded to better fit on top of your shoes. Be careful that the foam is not too hot when you are shaping this piece on your shoe. Hold the foam in the correct shape for a few minutes until it has cooled down. It will now hold its new shape. Repeat steps 1 through 3 for the other shoe. If you want to keep it simple, skip steps 4 and 5.

DECORATING THE EDGES

4. Measure the ½-inch (1-cm) wide strip of 2mm EVA foam along the edges of the armor pieces and cut it to the right lengths. To get neat corners, cut the strips diagonally where they need to connect. Leave the upper edge of the toe part free, since this will be covered with the instep layer, anyway. You will end up with six pieces of edging for each foot.

5. Glue the strips of foam to the foot armor around the edges. Where two ends of foam strips meet, glue these together so one continuous edge will form. Repeat these steps for the other foot.

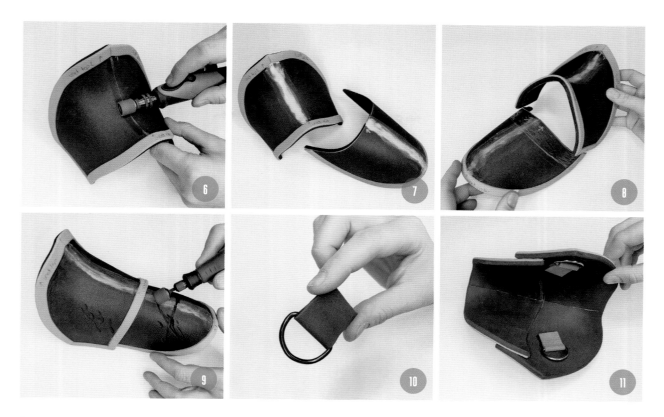

6. Using the rotary tool with 120-grit sanding drum, sand the edges of the foot armor layers so that the transition between the glued-on edges and the armor will get super smooth. Sand the glue seams smooth. The result of the sanding will look nicest when using a rotary tool, but you can also use regular sandpaper. Repeat this step for the other foot. After the sanding is done, clean the foam pieces by removing all of the dust.

OPTIONAL: SMOOTHING SEAMS WITH FILLER

7. If the seams are already smooth from the sanding, skip this step. Otherwise, to smooth out the seams even more, apply some filler on the seams, and smooth it out after adding some water to it (page 23). Leave the filler to dry overnight, and add more layers if necessary.

ASSEMBLING THE FOOT ARMOR

8. Try both layers of foot armor on your shoes while you wear them, and mark where you want the two pieces to overlap. Take it off and apply a thin layer of contact cement to both the top edge of the toe layer and the bottom edge of the instep layer. When the glue is tacky, connect both layers of the foot armor. Where you place the top layer on the bottom one will determine the ultimate shape of your armor piece. Repeat this for the other foot.

CREATING BATTLE DAMAGE

9. If you want to add battle damage, review the technique on page 24.

ADDING D-RINGS

10. Apply contact cement to both ends of the little strips of 2mm EVA foam. When the glue is almost dry, fold one foam strip through a D-ring and press it closed so the metal ring is attached. Repeat this for the rest of the D-rings.

11. Glue the piece of foam with the D-ring to the inside of the foot armor piece on the instep layer. Do this on both sides, so you can add an elastic strap here later. Repeat for the other foot.

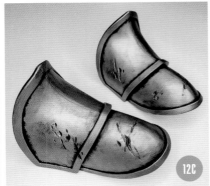

PRIMING AND PAINTING

12. Prime, paint and, optionally, protect the paint job with some varnish by using the technique from steps 13 through 15 from the Combat Helmet (pages 45 and 46).

MAKE IT WEARABLE

13. To figure out how long the piece of elastic needs to be to make the attachments, put the piece of elastic through both D-rings on one of the armor pieces. Put on the footwear that you want to wear with the armor, and try the foot armor piece on top of your shoe. Check the photos in step 15 to see how the elastic should wrap around your shoe. Mark how long the piece of elastic will need to be and cut it to size. Cut another piece of elastic in the same size for the other foot.

14. Fold the last ½ inch (1-cm) of both the ends of the elastic over, and sew the Velcro on top of those ends. You can also put some fabric glue underneath the fold and the Velcro before sewing to make the connection stronger.

Sew the hook part on one end of the elastic and the loop part on the other. Make sure that one is sewn on the top and the other on the bottom of the elastic, so the Velcro will function without having to twist the elastic. I used a sewing machine to sew this down, but you can also sew it by hand.

15. Pull the elastic strap through both D-rings on the foot armor pieces. To wear the foot armor, put the armor on top of your shoes and wrap one half of the elastic behind the heel and the other half underneath the arch of the foot. Close the Velcro in the back to secure it.

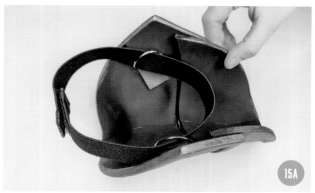

15A

15B

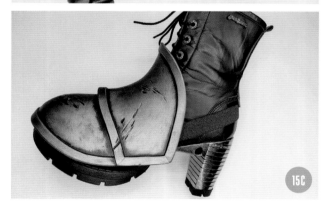

15C

Get Creative! Ideas for Variations

The shape of this armor piece is versatile and will fit with any costume design by simply painting it a different color. Add the horns from the Deadly Horned Pauldrons (page 59) on the toes of these foot armor pieces to make them look extra cool.

Foot armor can be hard to keep on the right spot sometimes while moving about. In this example, the elastic straps are worn underneath the arch of the foot and behind the heel, but it's possible that a different direction or spot for the straps will work better for your project. Try different positions to find the best solution.

If you don't like the elastic straps or just want to try something else, you can also sew some shoe covers for the footwear and sew some Velcro to it. Hot glue the other half of the Velcro to the inside of the armor piece, and you will be able to simply stick the armor on your shoes with the shoe covers while you are wearing them.

PROPS

TOOLS FOR ALL THREE PARTS OF THIS PROJECT

Hacksaw for cutting PVC pipe (optional)

Pliers and cutters for the metal wire

Paint marker

Craft knife

Cutting mat

Rotary tool with sanding drum (60- and 120-grit), or regular sandpaper

Woodburning tool or soldering iron

Heat gun

Safety tools, including a respirator, dust mask and safety glasses (review page 16)

Wooden clay modeling tool (optional)

Brushes and sponges for painting

Needle and thread

(continued)

ELVISH BOW, QUIVER AND ARROWS

With Branches of Golden Leaves

This bow with wood grain texture has branches with golden leaves vining around it. The combination of warm colors and natural textures makes this prop fit beautifully with any nature-loving character. The leather-looking quiver filled with arrows can be worn with a belt over the shoulders or at the hips and completes every ranger-style costume.

This prop consists of three projects: bow, arrows and quiver, and all the steps are divided in those mini projects to make it easier to follow.

MATERIALS FOR THE BOW

Bow templates (digital pattern plus pattern sheets I and II)

2 pieces of 0.6-inch (1.5-cm)-diameter PVC pipe

- Pipe A: 5½ inches (14 cm) long
- Pipe B: 3¼ inches (8.5 cm) long

1 pipe connector that fits the PVC pipes

8 feet (2.4 m) of metal wire (I used 1mm-diameter metal wire)

1 (24 x 20-inch [60 x 50-cm]) sheet of 6mm EVA foam

Contact cement

1 (12 x 6-inch [30 x 15-cm]) sheet of 2mm EVA foam

4 feet (1.2 m) of EVA foam prefab half-round dowel (I used 5mm wide, half-round dowel)

Foam clay

Flexible primer (black)

Acrylic paint (dark brown, light brown and beige)

Wax paint (I used Rub 'n Buff gold) or metallic acrylic paint

Oil paint (black) (optional)

Matte and glossy (spray) varnish (optional)

1 thin strip of jersey fabric (mine was 3 feet [1 m] long in moss green)

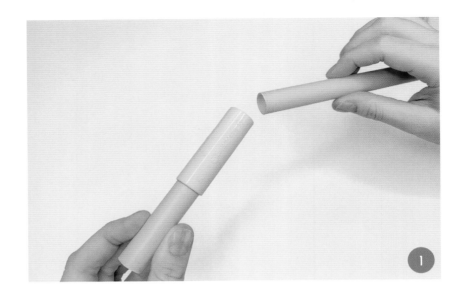

The Bow

PREPARATION

If not already cut to size, use a saw to cut the 0.6-inch (1.5-cm)-diameter PVC pipe into a 5½-inch (14-cm)-long piece of pipe and a 3¼-inch (8.5-cm)-long piece.

Cut the metal wire into two equal pieces. Metal wire gauges can differ per country, and the thickness is not super important for this project, so just pick one that you can find. Just keep in mind that the wire needs to be sturdy, but still bendy enough so you can twist it without having to use much force.

Use the templates to trace and cut all the layers for the bow base out of the 6mm EVA foam.

Cut two (3 x 3-inch [8 x 8-cm]) squares out of the 6mm EVA foam.

Use the 2mm EVA foam to cut four (4¼ x 1½-inch [11 x 4-cm]) strips, one (4¼ x 2½-inch [11 x 6-cm]) strip and one (2½ x 2½-inch [6 x 6-cm]) square. These will all be used for the grip.

BUILDING THE GRIP

1. Take the pieces of PVC pipes and the PVC connector. Glue the PVC connector to the shorter PVC pipe piece (pipe B). Instead of waiting for the contact cement to get tacky like usual, put the two pieces together immediately while the glue is still wet. This is important because if you wait for the glue to become tacky, you won't be able to put the connector over the pipe because the glue will prevent it.

Note: The PVC pipe connector is used so the bow can be taken apart into two pieces for easier storage/traveling. You can skip the connector and use one long piece of PVC pipe if you don't mind the size of the complete prop.

2. Glue the 4¼ x 2½-inch (11 x 6-cm) and the 2½ x 2½-inch (6 x 6-cm) pieces of 2mm EVA foam around the PVC pipes, avoiding the connector. Also apply contact cement to where the two ends of the EVA foam connect, so you have one continuous surface of EVA foam.

3. Glue the two squares of 6mm EVA foam around the two parts of the bow grip. Where the two ends of the EVA foam connect, apply some contact cement so one continuous surface of EVA foam will form. If the pieces of foam are too long, cut a bit off until they fit snugly around the bow grip.

MATERIALS FOR FOUR ARROWS

Arrows templates (digital pattern)

1 (18 x 8-inch [45 x 20-cm]) sheet of 6mm EVA foam

1 (10 x 6-inch [25 x 15-cm]) piece of 2mm EVA foam

4 (24-inch [60-cm]-long) 8mm-diameter wooden sticks

Contact cement

Flexible primer (black)

Acrylic paint (dark brown, light brown, beige and silver)

Matte and satin (spray) varnish (optional)

MATERIALS FOR THE QUIVER

Quiver templates (pattern sheets II and VI)

1 (19½ x 16-inch [50 x 40-cm]) sheet of 6mm EVA foam

1 (18 x 10-inch [45 x 25-cm]) piece of 10mm EVA foam

Contact cement

Filler (optional)

Foam clay

Flexible primer (black)

Acrylic paint (dark brown and light brown)

Wax paint (I used Rub 'n Buff gold) or metallic acrylic paint

Matte and glossy (spray) varnish (optional)

3 thin strips of jersey fabric (mine were 5 feet [1.5 m] long in moss green)

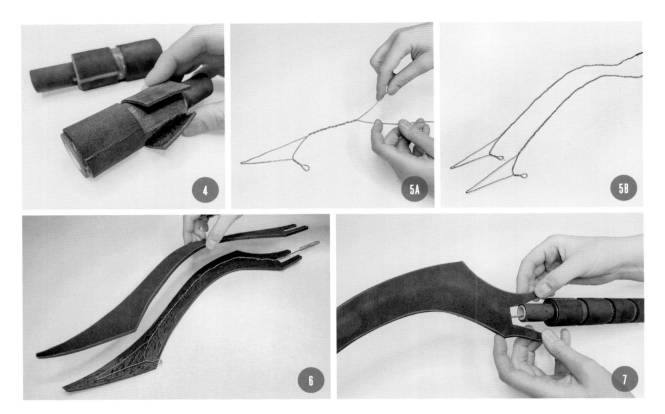

4. Glue the four thin strips of 2mm EVA foam around the grip. Make sure to space them out evenly with a bit of distance between each. Where the two ends of the EVA foam connect, apply some contact cement so one continuous surface of EVA foam will form.

CONSTRUCTING THE LIMBS OF THE BOW

5. Fold one of the pieces of metal wire in half. Use the pliers to form a loop at the end, which will be used to tie the string to later. Also form the shape of the end of the bow limb with the metal wire. Twist the rest of the wire to make it one thicker and stronger piece. The guideline on the template can help to get the wire in the correct shape.

6. Apply a thin layer of contact cement to the two 6mm pieces of the first layer of the limb. When the glue is tacky, put the twisted and shaped metal wire on top of one foam piece and then press the other foam piece on top of it to secure the metal wire between the foam pieces.

7. Apply contact cement to the grip of the bow around the foam on the tip. Also apply contact cement on the inside of the opening on the base of the limb. When the glue is tacky, attach the limb over the tip of the grip. Make sure it's in the middle.

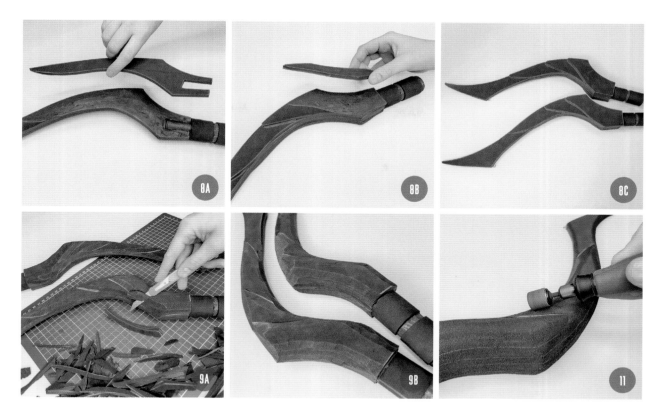

8. Take the remaining layers that you cut for the bow limbs and glue them on the limbs. Start with the second layer, then the third and end with the fourth (top) layer. The thickest part of the bow, which is closest to the grip, will consist of eight layers of foam when you are done stacking. Repeat these steps for the second limb of the bow.

SHAPING THE BOW

9. With a sharp craft knife, carve the limbs of the bow into a rounder, organic shape. This doesn't need to be perfect, because it will be sanded smooth later.

10. Using the rotary tool with 60-grit sanding drum, sand the limbs of the bow further into shape and start smoothing it out.

11. Switch the sanding drum for a finer one (120-grit), and sand the limbs of the bow smooth.

The result of the sanding will look nicest when using a rotary tool, but you can also use regular sandpaper. After the sanding is done, clean the foam pieces by removing all of the dust.

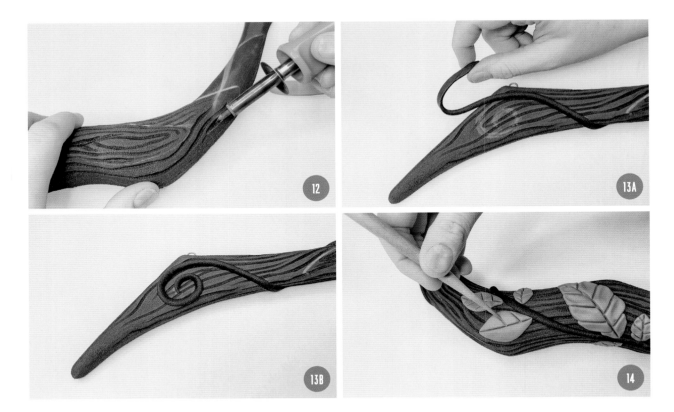

ADDING WOOD GRAIN TEXTURE

12. If you want to add a wood grain texture to the limbs of the bow, use the same technique in step 6 from the Deadly Horned Pauldrons (page 61).

ADD STEMS AND FOAM CLAY LEAVES

13. Decide where you want the stems for the decorative leaves to go and mark them with a paint marker on the foam. I made the stems swirl around the bow's limbs, but you can make any shape you want with them. Apply the stems to the bow by using the technique in steps 9 and 10 from the Layered Elven Bracers (page 86).

After adding the stems, heat the whole bow with the heat gun to heat-seal it and close the pores of the foam. Be careful not to heat the PVC pipe too much because it can melt under the heat, making the connection malfunction.

14. Add foam clay leaves by using the technique in steps 11 and 12 from the Layered Elven Bracers (pages 86 and 87).

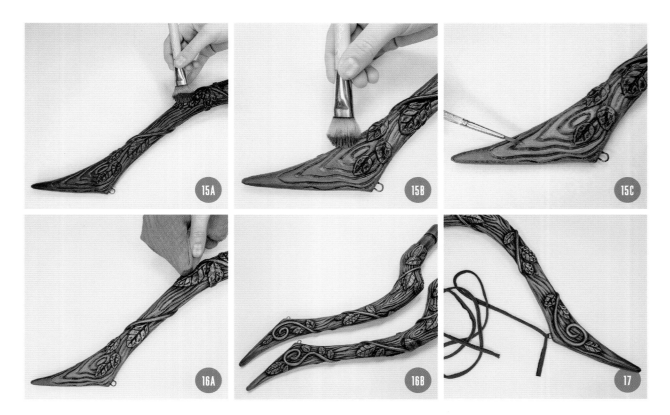

PRIMING AND PAINTING

15. Apply primer and paint and create highlights on the wood grain texture by using the techniques in steps 10 through 12 from the Deadly Horned Pauldrons (page 62).

16. To paint the stems and the leaves, and, optionally, protect the entire paint job, review the technique used in steps 16 through 18 from the Layered Elven Bracers (page 88). Optionally, apply some black oil paint to the edges around the stems and leaves that could use some shadows. Apply with a thin brush first, and then, with a larger, fluffier brush, blend the wet paint out in a nice gradient.

Note: If you applied the oil paint shadows, go for the spray varnish to coat the whole piece. Oil paint dries very slowly and it can take multiple weeks to dry. So, if you apply a brush-on varnish, you could smear out the oil paint in this step. The glossy varnish in the end can still be applied with a brush.

ADD THE STRING

17. To finish the bow, tie the piece of jersey fabric to both of the metal wire loops that are sticking out of the limbs of the bow at the ends. Secure the knot by hand sewing a few stitches with needle and thread if you like. The bow is now ready to be used with a costume!

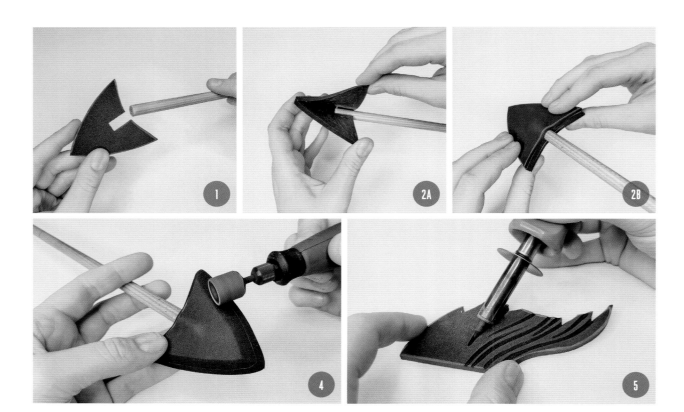

The Arrows

PREPARATION

Cut the arrowhead four times out of the 6mm EVA foam. Cut the arrow fletching eight times out of the 6mm EVA foam.

Use the 2mm EVA foam to cut the arrowhead eight times.

THE ARROWHEAD

1. Glue the 6mm EVA foam arrowhead to the end of one stick.

2. Glue a 2mm-thick arrowhead piece to both sides of one 6mm-thick arrowhead, to create a thicker arrowhead and to cover the end of the stick completely with foam.

3. Using the rotary tool with 60-grit sanding drum, sand the arrowhead's edges down into a pointy end and start smoothing it out.

4. Switch the sanding drum for a finer one (120-grit), and sand the edges of the arrowhead smooth. The result of the sanding will look nicest when using a rotary tool, but you can also use regular sandpaper. After the sanding is done, clean the foam piece by removing all of the dust.

THE FLETCHING

5. Turn on your woodburning tool and when it's heated up, start burning lines into the foam for the two pieces of the fletching to create texture. Press harder to create deeper, thicker lines or gentler for narrower, thinner lines. Add this texture to the front and back of the pieces.

6. Glue both fletching pieces to the sides of the bare tip of the wooden stick. Repeat these steps for the other three arrows, and make even more arrows if you want!

PRIMING AND PAINTING

7. Prepare the arrows for priming and painting by heat-sealing the foam parts.

Apply a flexible primer onto the arrow and cover it completely (the foam and the wood). I used two layers of Hex-Flex black. Leave the primer to dry for 2 to 4 hours.

8. Apply a layer of brown acrylic paint to the arrow fletching and stick. Make sure to leave the texture lines on the fletching pieces black by only painting on the raised parts. Also leave the arrowhead black.

9. Using a lighter brown, apply a thin layer of paint on the raised areas of the fletching pieces to create some highlights.

10. Apply some beige acrylic paint to the tips of the fletching to create more highlights. Leave the highlight layer of paint to dry for 1 to 2 hours.

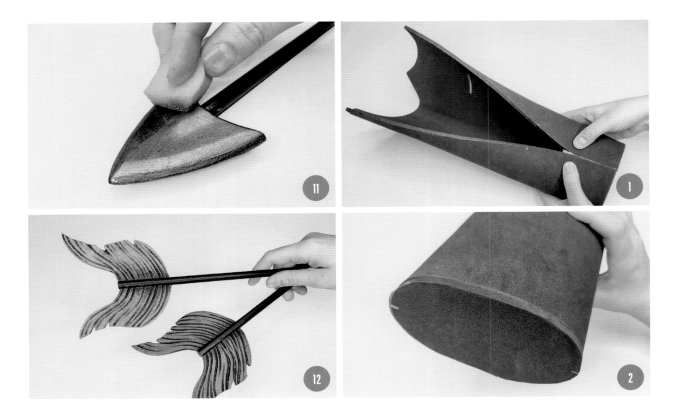

11. Apply silver acrylic paint on the arrowhead. (I used Dark Silver from HexFlex.) Dab it on with a sponge, to prevent brushstrokes. Acrylic metallic paint usually dries really quickly, so leave it to dry for 1 hour.

12. Leave the paint job to fully dry overnight, and then optionally add a layer of varnish to protect it. Either spray or paint over the paint with a matte acrylic varnish. Leave the varnish to dry for 2 to 4 hours. Add a satin varnish to the arrowheads if you want those to have a bit more shine.

The Quiver

PREPARATION

Cut the quiver base and bottom out of the 6mm EVA foam.

Cut the decorative bands out of the 10mm EVA foam.

BUILDING THE BASE

1. Apply contact cement to both side edges of the quiver. When the glue is tacky, bend the foam and connect the two edges to form a hollow tube.

2. Apply contact cement to the underside of the quiver and to the edge of the bottom. When the glue is tacky, press the bottom to the quiver. If you want to keep the quiver plain, skip steps 3 and 8 through 11 to leave the detailing off.

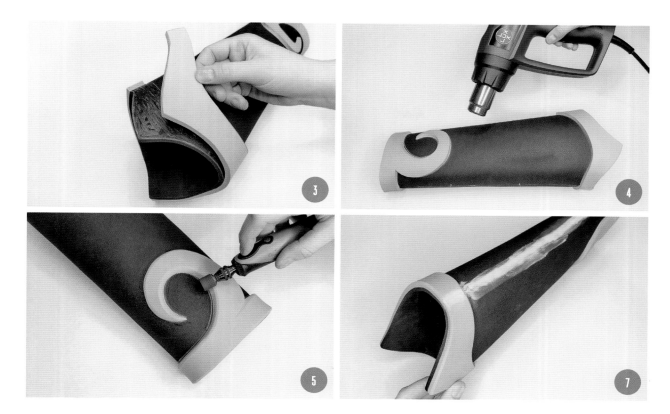

ADDING DECORATIVE EDGING

3. Glue the 10mm decorative edges around the quiver. Apply contact cement where the two ends of the decorations meet to form one continuous edge. Do this for the top and bottom edge of the quiver.

SHAPING AND REFINING THE QUIVER

4. Heat the quiver with the heat gun. When the foam is hot, press the quiver on both sides and shape it to be a bit more oval so it will feel more comfortable when wearing it against the body. Hold the quiver for a few minutes in this oval shape until it's cooled down, so the foam will stay in this shape.

5. Using the rotary tool with 60-grit sanding drum, sand the decorative edges so they are more rounded.

6. Switch the sanding drum for a finer one (120-grit), and sand the edges of the decorative shapes smooth. Also sand the glue seams. The result of the sanding will look nicest when using a rotary tool, but you can also use regular sandpaper. After the sanding is done, clean the foam piece by removing all of the dust.

7. If these seams are already nice and smooth from the sanding, skip this step. Otherwise, you can smooth them even more by applying filler to the seams and smoothing it out after adding some water to it (page 23). Leave the filler to dry overnight, and add more layers if necessary.

After this step, heat the whole quiver with the heat gun to heat-seal it and close the pores of the foam.

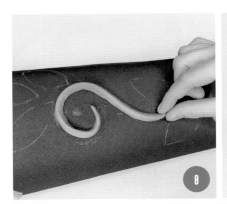

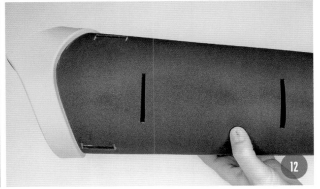

MAKING FOAM CLAY FOLIAGE

8. Take a bit of foam clay out of the pot and form it into a roll. If the foam clay is too dry, mix some water into it.

Using your fingers, apply a little bit of water to the quiver where you want the stem for the leaves. This will help the foam clay stick better to the foam. Pinch the roll of clay into a triangular bevel shape, place it on the quiver and press it down a bit. Press the edges down on the foam, so it will adhere better to the quiver.

9. With some foam clay, form a small flat leaf shape and put it on your working surface. (I used a silicone mat.) With a wooden clay modeling tool, carve lines in the leaf to look like veins.

10. Apply a little bit of water to the quiver where you want to place the leaf. Then place the leaf shape on the quiver and press it down a bit.

11. On the edges of the leaf, push the foam clay outwards softly, using a rounder clay modeling tool to give some more shape to the leaf. I made five leaves, but you can add as many leaves as you want, following these steps. Set the project aside for 24 to 48 hours so the foam clay can air-dry.

HOLES FOR THE STRAP

12. On the back of the quiver, cut some rectangular-shaped holes in the foam for the strap to go through. Cut two horizontal holes if you want to wear the quiver on your back, or cut two vertical holes if you want to wear the quiver on your hip. Or keep both options open by cutting all four of these holes, like I did.

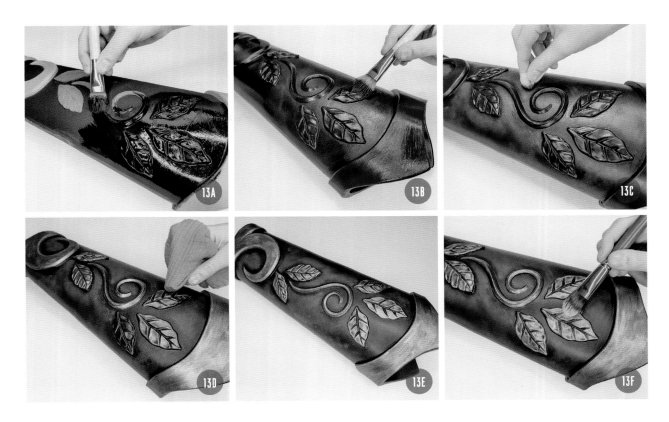

PRIMING AND PAINTING

13. Prime, paint and, optionally, protect the quiver using steps 13 through 18 from the Layered Elven Bracers (pages 87 and 88).

Get Creative! Ideas for Variations

For the Bow: Make the bow's silhouette even more interesting by adding some spikes or horns with foam clay, or you can even use the horns from the Deadly Horned Pauldrons (page 59).

I used a piece of jersey fabric for the string, but you can substitute this for a piece of elastic.

For the Arrows: If you want a large number of arrows sticking out from the quiver, it can get quite crowded with all the arrowheads, so I recommend crafting some dummy arrows that only have the fletching. That way you can fit a lot of "arrows" in the quiver!

For the Quiver: Instead of using braided straps for the quiver, it can also be worn on a belt. Use your imagination to come up with interesting designs to decorate the quiver to make it totally unique and personalized. I bet some elvish knotwork would look so beautiful!

MAKE IT WEARABLE

14. Braid the three long strips of jersey fabric. Close the two ends of the braid with some hand stitches with needle and thread so they won't come undone.

15. Pull the strap through the holes in the back of the quiver. You can wear the quiver on your back with the strap over your shoulder, or on your hip with the strap around your waist.

MATERIALS

Knight's Shining Sword templates (pattern sheets II and III)

1 (37½-inch [95-cm]-long) ¼-inch (6-mm)-diameter fiberglass rod or wooden stick

1 (36 x 10-inch [90 x 25-cm]) sheet of 6mm EVA foam

1 (18 x 18-inch [45 x 45-cm]) sheet of 10mm EVA foam

1 (8 x 6-inch [20 x 15-cm]) piece of 2mm EVA foam

Contact cement

Foam clay

12 inches (30 cm) of EVA foam prefab half-round dowel (I used 5mm wide)

Flexible primer (black)

Acrylic paint (dark brown, light brown and silver)

Oil paint (black) (optional)

Satin and matte (spray) varnish (optional)

TOOLS

Paint marker

Craft knife

Cutting mat

Heat gun

Safety tools, including a respirator, dust mask and safety glasses (review page 16)

Rotary tool with sanding drums (60- and 120-grit), or regular sandpaper

Wooden clay modeling tool (optional)

Brushes and sponges for painting

KNIGHT'S SHINING SWORD
With Decorated Guard and Pommel

This silver sword is a cool prop that isn't too difficult to make and will fit with many costumes.

The handle of the sword is long enough to hold with two hands, but the sword is so lightweight that it can also be used singlehandedly and be combined with the Protective Shield (page 173). The sword can be combined with a full armor costume, but it also looks awesome with a basic medieval-style tunic or dress. If you want to look even more epic in a photoshoot, build two of these so you can be double-wielding these swords!

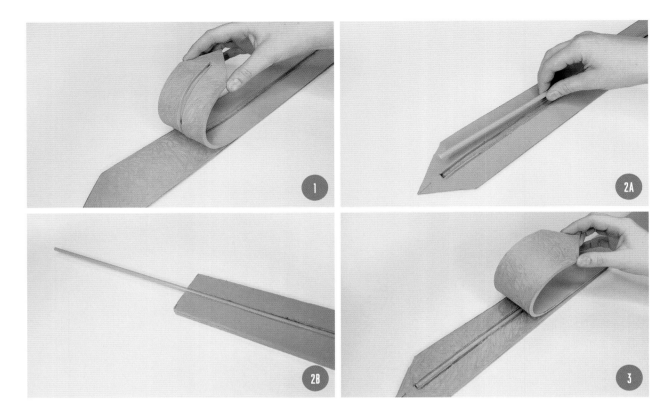

PREPARATION

Before cutting the foam, decide how long you want the sword to be. This can depend on the length of your rod/stick or on the character design. My sword is a total length of roughly 40 inches (100 cm). If that sounds good to you, then simply use the templates like they are. But if you want to make it shorter or longer, adjust the template accordingly before cutting the foam.

Cut the three layers for the blade out of the 6mm EVA foam.

Cut the layers for the grip out of the 6mm and 10mm EVA foam.

Use the 10mm EVA foam to cut out the layers for the guard. For the pommel, use both the 10mm and 6mm foam.

Cut two strips out of the 6mm EVA foam: one (4¾ x ¾-inch [12 x 2-cm]) and one (4¼ x ½-inch [11 x 1-cm]). These strips will be used to decorate the grip.

From the 2mm EVA foam, cut out the details for decorating the guard, twice.

BUILDING THE BLADE

1. Lay one of the blade layers without the slit on the table. Apply a thin layer of contact cement to both the bottom layer and the layer with the slit in the middle, and when the glue is tacky, attach them together.

2. Apply some contact cement inside the slit and place the rod in the middle of the slit. Notice that there is a part of the rod sticking out. That is where the grip of the sword will be.

3. Glue the third blade layer to the top of the middle layer and the rod.

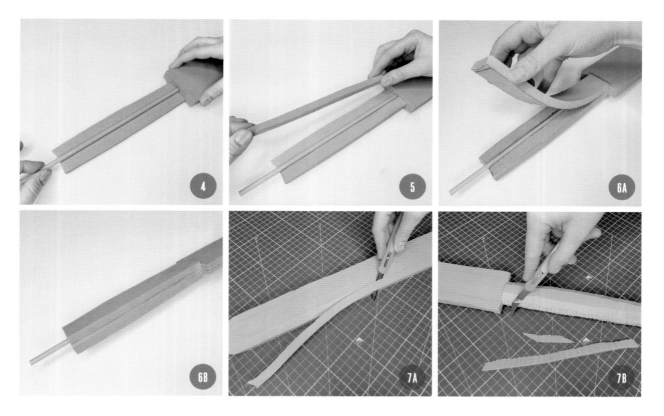

BUILDING THE GRIP

4. Gather the four pieces for the grip. Apply contact cement to one of the 10mm-thick layers for the grip, and when the glue is tacky, attach the piece of foam to the rod. Make sure to also apply glue to the edges where the grip piece connects to the blade to make a strong connection.

5. Take the 6mm EVA foam pieces for the middle layer of the grip and glue them on top of the bottom layer, on both sides of the rod.

6. Glue the other 10mm-thick layer for the grip on top. Make sure to also apply glue to the edges where this grip piece connects to the blade.

Notice that there is still a part of the rod sticking out. This is where the pommel will be attached.

SHAPING THE BLADE AND GRIP

7. With a sharp craft knife, carve foam away from the edges of the sword's blade so it will be beveled.

Also carve the grip into an oval, rounded shape. This doesn't need to be perfect because it will be sanded smooth later.

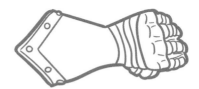

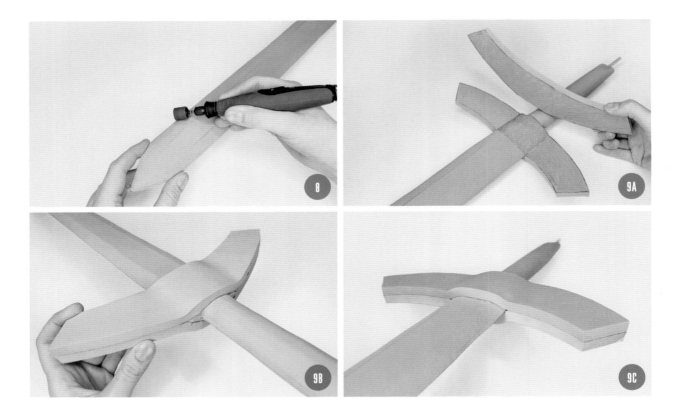

8. Using the rotary tool with 60-grit sanding drum, sand the blade's edge and the grip further into shape. To get the blade nice and straight, it helps to draw straight lines on the foam to mark how far you want to sand. Switch the sanding drum for a finer one (120-grit), and sand the edges of the blade and the grip smooth. The result of the sanding will look nicest when using a rotary tool, but you can also use regular sandpaper. After the sanding is done, clean the foam pieces by removing all of the dust.

BUILD THE POMMEL AND THE GUARD

9. Now that the blade and grip are smooth, glue one 10mm-thick half of the guard on the blade just above the grip. The beveled edge of the blade will help shape the guard nicely.

Then flip the sword upside down and glue the other half of the guard to it.

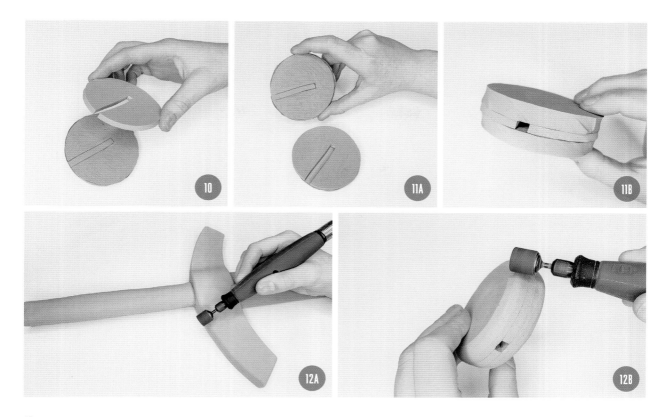

10. Gather the three pieces for the pommel. Trace the slit mark on the 6mm-thick circle onto both of the 10mm-thick circles to mark where the glue will go. Lay one of the 10mm-thick circles on the table and glue the 6mm-thick circle on top. Make sure to keep the slit area free of glue, otherwise it will be hard to pull the pommel over the rod later.

11. Take the top layer for the pommel and glue it to the middle layer. Again, make sure to keep the slit free of glue.

SHAPING THE POMMEL AND GUARD

12. Using the rotary tool with 120-grit sanding drum, sand the edges of the guard and the pommel smooth. Also sand the sides smooth to hide where the layers were glued together.

The result of the sanding will look nicest when using a rotary tool, but you can also use regular sandpaper. After the sanding is done, clean the foam piece by removing all of the dust.

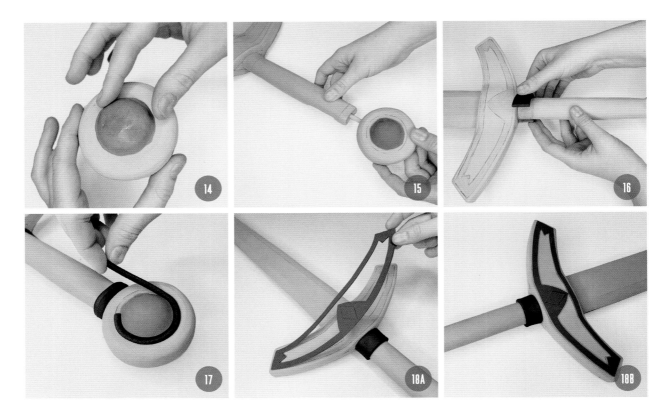

DECORATING THE SWORD

13. Take a bit of foam clay out of the pot and form a flat round shape with it. If the foam clay is too dry, mix some water into it. Using your fingers, apply a little bit of water on the side of the pommel where you want to place the decoration. This will make the foam clay stick better to the foam.

14. Press the round clay shape softly onto the pommel and push the sides down until it has a cabochon shape. Use your fingers to do the sculpting and optionally, some wooden clay modeling tools. Now leave the project aside for 24 to 48 hours so the foam clay can air-dry. It doesn't matter if your sphere isn't perfectly shaped right now since it will get a bit puffier once the foam clay has air-dried. When the foam clay is dry, turn the pommel around and repeat the steps on the other side, adding another foam clay round shape to the pommel. Leave the project aside for another 24 to 48 hours so the foam clay can air-dry.

15. When the foam clay shapes are air dried, apply some contact cement inside the hole in the pommel and also on the edge of the pommel where it will be connected to the grip, and on the edge of the grip and the rod. Instead of waiting for the glue to get tacky, immediately put the pommel over the tip of the rod and press it firmly into the edge of the grip.

16. Take the two strips of 6mm EVA foam and glue these around the grip. The wider strip goes against the guard, and the thinner strip goes against the pommel. If you like these strips to have rounded edges, you can also sand the edges smooth using the rotary tool with 120-grit sanding drum.

17. Take the half-round foam dowel, lay it around the foam clay shape and cut it to the right length. Glue the dowel around the foam clay shape to create extra detail. Repeat this for the foam clay shape on the other side.

18. Take the 2mm shapes that you cut out to decorate the guard. Place them on the guard to mark where you will need to apply glue, and then glue them down. Also, glue the little diamond shapes on top of the details as an extra layer of detailing.

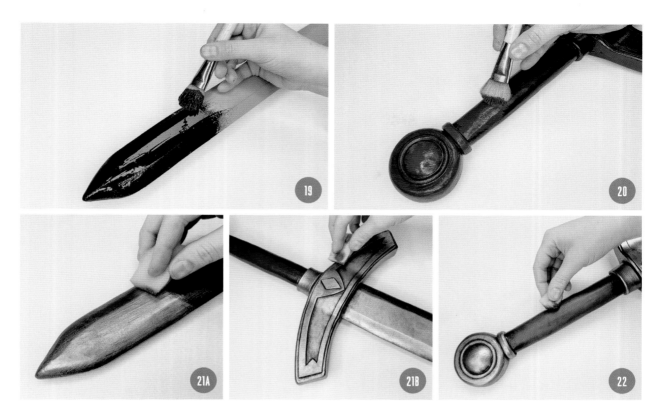

PRIMING AND PAINTING

19. Prepare the piece for priming and painting by heat-sealing it with a heat gun.

Apply a flexible primer onto the entire piece. I used two layers of HexFlex black. Leave the primer to dry for 2 to 4 hours.

20. Apply a layer of dark brown acrylic paint on the grip to start making it look like leather. Add more paint to the middle part and less paint on the edges where shadows naturally occur. If your primer wasn't black, then you can also add some black paint on the shadow parts. Leave the brown paint to dry for two to four hours.

Note: I also painted the pommel brown by mistake, but that is not needed if you want to paint it silver. If you want to paint it gold, then by all means, paint it all brown now.

21. Apply silver acrylic paint to the blade, the guard and the pommel. (I used Dark Silver from HexFlex.) Dab it on with a sponge, instead of a brush, to prevent brushstrokes. Put only a little bit of paint on the sponge each time, and try to stay away from corners so the black shadow color can still show through. If you managed to keep the shadows dark, and get a nice gradient in this step already, you can skip step 23. Acrylic metallic paint usually dries really quickly, so leave it to dry for 1 hour.

22. Apply the light brown color with a sponge to the grip, to create more depth.

23. If you want to take the paint job to the next level, apply some black oil paint to the edges on the piece that could use some shadows. Apply with a thin brush first, and then with a larger, fluffier brush, blend the still wet paint out in a nice gradient. You can also use black acrylic paint for this.

24. Leave the paint job to fully dry overnight, and then optionally add a layer of varnish to protect it. Either spray or paint over the paint with a satin acrylic varnish. I used a satin acrylic spray varnish and applied one layer. Leave it to dry overnight.

Note: If you applied the oil paint shadows, go for the spray varnish to coat the whole piece. Since oil paint dries very slowly and it can take multiple weeks to dry, using a brush-on varnish could smear the oil paint in this step.

25. After the satin varnish is dry, optionally apply a layer of matte varnish over the grip to make it look more like leather. Leave the varnish to dry overnight. The sword is now ready to use as a prop with your costumes!

MATERIALS

Protective Shield templates (pattern sheets IV and V)

1 (31½ x 18-inch [80 x 45-cm]) sheet of 6mm EVA foam

1 (21½ x 16-inch [55 x 40-cm]) sheet of 10mm EVA foam

55 inches (1.4 m) of 1-inch (2.5-cm)-wide 2mm EVA foam

Contact cement

1 (2 x 2-inch [5 x 5-cm]) piece of 2mm EVA foam

Flexible primer (black)

Acrylic paint (dark brown, gold, dark gold and silver)

Oil paint (black) (optional)

Satin and glossy (spray) varnish (optional)

TOOLS

Paint marker

Craft knife

Cutting mat

Heat gun

Safety tools, including a respirator, dust mask and safety glasses (review page 16)

Rotary tool with sanding drum (120-grit), or regular sandpaper

Measuring tape

Brushes and sponges for

PROTECTIVE SHIELD
With Coat of Arms Decoration

This epic shield is just perfect for a knight costume, and paired with the Knight's Shining Sword (page 165), you'll have a perfect ensemble. The rounded shape of the shield is acquired by gluing two layers of foam together while they are held in a curve. This is a great method for shaping such big items. The middle of the shield draws the attention with a big lily decoration. The rays of light that radiate from this lily are painted in a different shade of gold to bring more depth and variation to the full look of the shield.

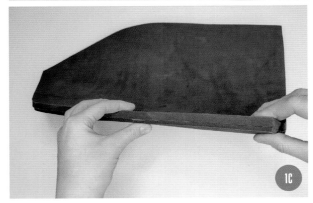

PREPARATION

Cut the slightly wider version of the shield base out of the 6mm EVA foam, and cut the slightly narrower version out of the 10mm EVA foam. The different widths will be important to get the curve in the shield.

Use the 6mm EVA foam to cut three ½-inch (1-cm)-wide strips, two that are 20 inches (51 cm) long and one that is 12½ inches (32 cm) long. Also cut the parts for the lily detail and the corner decorations out of the 6mm foam.

Cut the grip out of the 10mm EVA foam.

Use the small piece of 2mm EVA foam to cut five circles that are ½ inch (1.5 cm) in diameter.

BUILDING THE BASE

1. Heat the 10mm shield base piece with the heat gun. When the foam is hot, shape it to give it a curve. Hold the foam in this curve for a few minutes until it cools down, so it will keep the new shape. Heat-shaping the foam is not necessary, but it will make it easier to glue the second layer on, while keeping the curved shape.

Apply a thin layer of contact cement to both shield base pieces. Since these surfaces are rather big, try to work fast. Use a scrap piece of foam or a spatula to spread out the glue over the foam as evenly as possible.

When you finish applying glue to both pieces, the glue will probably already be tacky where you started because it's such a big surface. Start at one of the sides to place the two layers together. The thinner foam needs to go on top of the thicker foam. Make sure to keep the bottom layer curved while you glue the second layer on.

When you finish putting the layers together, press firmly on the sides so the foam is connected well and to avoid having gaps in the sides. It is OK if the sides are not completely aligned, because you can sand that smooth later.

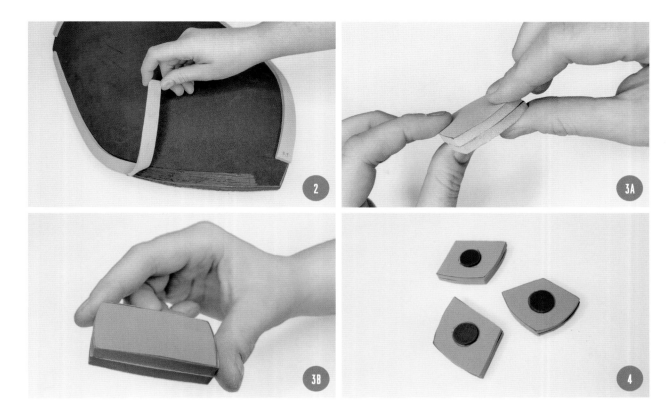

DECORATING THE EDGES

2. Lay the three 10mm corner decorations on the top side of the shield (the side made of the 6mm foam), and mark where they will go, then set them aside. Now take the three thin strips of 6mm EVA foam and check if they are the right length to fit on all the three edges of the shield, without touching where the corner decorations will go. Cut the pieces shorter if needed, and then glue them on the edges of the shield.

PREPARING THE CORNER AND LILY DECORATIONS

3. Assemble the corner decorations by taking the two layers for each of the three corners and stacking them together with contact cement to create a thicker decoration.

Assemble the middle part of the lily decoration by gluing the two layers together.

4. Take three of the 2mm circles and glue them to the corner decorations. Glue the two remaining circles on either end of the shield grip.

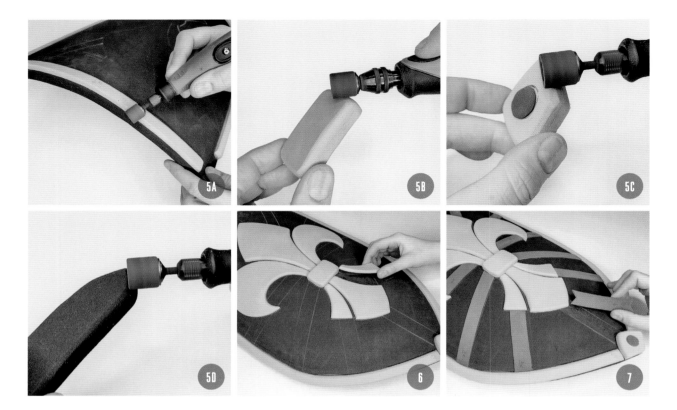

CLEANING UP THE EDGES

5. Using the rotary tool with 120-grit sanding drum, sand the edges of the shield smooth. The transition between the glued together layers will get super smooth in this step.

Also sand the edges of all the pieces for the lily decoration and the corner decorations, but make sure to only sand the sides and top, and leave the bottoms flat. Sand all the edges of the shield grip smooth. The result of the sanding will look nicest when using a rotary tool, but you can also use regular sandpaper. After the sanding is done, clean the foam pieces by removing all of the dust.

DECORATING THE SHIELD

6. Before you start gluing the lily pieces on, measure where the middle of the shield is and sketch some lines. Then glue the smooth lily pieces on. Also glue on the corner decorations between the decorative edging.

7. Cut the 1-inch (2.5-cm)-wide strip of 2mm EVA foam into the right lengths. Put the strips on the foam where you want to place the rays of sunshine detailing, mark how long they need to be and cut them to the right lengths. Mark them with letters so you won't mix them up when gluing them onto the shield. Now, glue them on the shield.

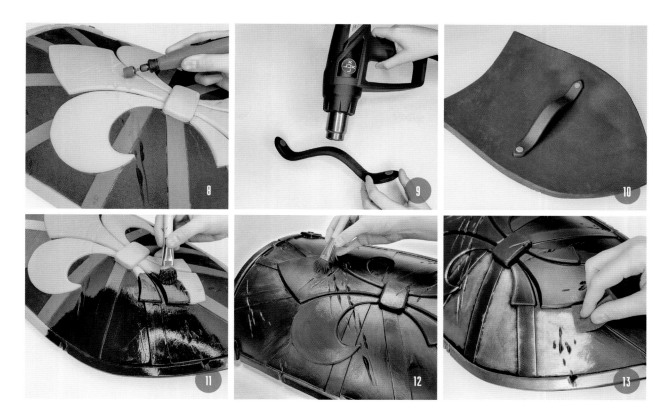

CREATING BATTLE DAMAGE

8. If you want to add battle damage to the shield, review the technique on page 24.

ADDING THE GRIP TO THE BACK

9. Heat the grip with a heat gun. When the foam is hot, shape it with some curves so it will fit on the back of the shield. Hold the grip in the curved shape for a few minutes until the foam has cooled down, so it will stay in that shape.

10. Hold the shield in front of you how you would like to hold it and decide where, and in which direction, you want the grip. Then glue both ends of the grip onto the back of the shield. I put mine horizontal, below the middle of the shield.

PRIMING AND PAINTING

11. Prepare the shield for priming and painting by heat-sealing with a heat gun.

When the foam is cooled down again, apply a flexible primer onto the shield. Cover the complete front and back of the shield. I used two layers of HexFlex black. Leave the primer to dry for 2 to 4 hours.

12. Apply some dark brown acrylic paint on the lily decorations and the sunrays. This will serve as a good shadow color for gold. Leave it to dry for 2 to 4 hours.

13. Apply silver acrylic paint on the shield. (I used Dark Silver from HexFlex.) Dab it on with a sponge to prevent brushstrokes. Put only a little bit of paint on the sponge each time, and try to stay away from the corners and the battle damage dents so the black shadow color still shows through. Acrylic metallic paint usually dries really quickly, so leave it to dry for 1 hour.

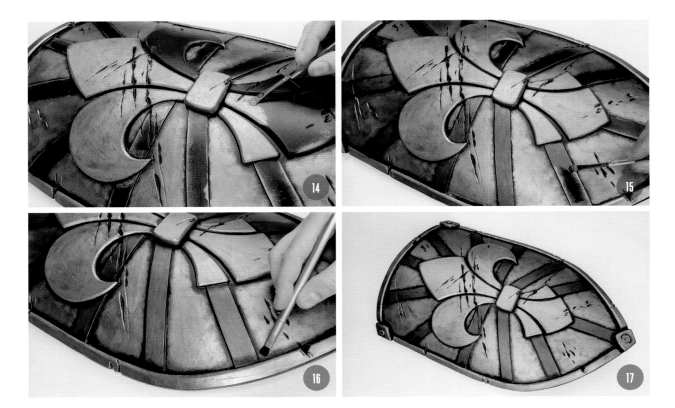

14. Apply some gold metallic acrylic paint on the lily decoration (I used 14kg Gold from Cospaint.) Only paint the raised surface, and not the shadows, to give it even more depth. Leave it to dry for 1 hour.

15. Apply a darker color of gold metallic acrylic paint to the sunrays. (I used Espresso Gold from Cospaint.)

16. If you want to take your paint job to the next level, apply some black oil paint to the edges that could use some shadows. Apply with a thin brush first, and then with a larger, fluffier brush, blend the still wet paint out in a nice gradient. You can also use black acrylic paint for this. If the shadows already look good and the paint job doesn't need cleaning up, then simply skip this step.

17. Leave the paint job to fully dry overnight and then optionally add a layer of varnish to protect it. Either spray or paint over the paint with a satin acrylic varnish. I used a satin acrylic spray varnish and applied one layer. Leave to dry overnight.

Note: If you applied the oil paint shadows, go for the spray varnish to coat the whole piece. Oil paint dries very slowly and it can take multiple weeks to dry, so you might smear the oil paint if you apply with a brush-on varnish.

Get Creative! Ideas for Variations

Swap out the lily decoration for your own design or try out different shapes. A rounded shield would be great for a Viking character, or make it rectangular for a Roman-style shield.

Add a wood grain texture to the shield instead to make it look like it is crafted out of wood.

If you make this shield for a child, you can make it smaller so they can hold it.

MATERIALS

Magic Spellbook templates (digital pattern plus pattern sheet II)

1 (10 x 8-inch [25 x 20-cm]) sheet of 10mm EVA foam

1 (18 x 14-inch [45 x 35-cm]) sheet of 6mm EVA foam

1 (8 x 6-inch [20 x 15-cm]) piece of 2mm EVA foam

Contact cement

48 inches (120 cm) of EVA foam prefab half-round dowel (I used 10mm wide)

8 inches (20 cm) of EVA foam prefab half-round dowel (I used 15mm wide)

Flexible primer (black)

Acrylic paint (dark brown, white, blue, silver and gold)

Matte and glossy varnish (optional)

TOOLS

Paint marker

Craft knife

Cutting mat

Heat gun

Safety tools, including a respirator, dust mask and safety glasses (review page 16)

Woodburning tool or soldering iron

Rotary tool with sanding drum (120-grit), or regular sandpaper

Brushes for painting

MAGIC SPELLBOOK
With Sun and Moon Decorations

This hefty tome of spells is a great beginner-friendly project to craft for a sorceress or wizard costume. The book is bound in blue "leather" and decorated with a shining sun on one side and a moon and stars on the other. The book looks like it has pages, but in reality, the sides are made of EVA foam that has texture lines burned into it with a woodburning tool. So the book is completely hollow, making it really lightweight.

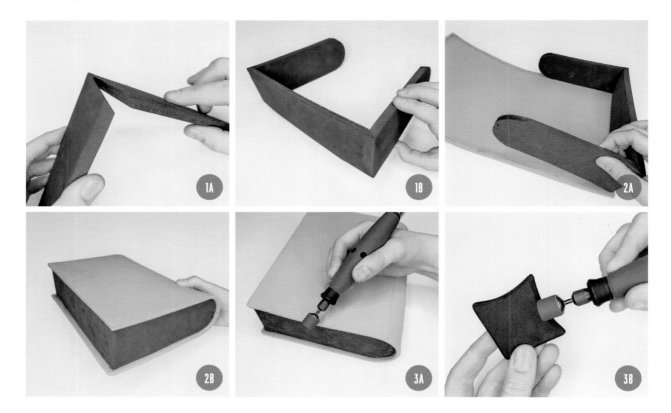

PREPARATION

Use your template to trace and cut the pieces for the pages out of the 10mm EVA foam. Make sure to check the template for the markings, and cut some of the edges at an angle.

Cut the book cover and the corner decorations out of the 6mm EVA foam.

Use the 2mm EVA foam to cut the moon, sun and other decorations.

BUILDING THE BASE SHAPE

1. Apply a thin layer of contact cement to the three 10mm pieces for the pages on the angled corners. When the glue is tacky, connect the pieces together to form the top, side and bottom edges of the book.

2. Now take the cover of the book and place it over and around the pages to see where you will need to apply the glue, and mark it with a paint marker. Apply the glue on both the cover of the book and edge of the pages. When the glue is tacky, put the pages on top of one side of the cover.

Then bend the book cover over the pages and press it there until the cover is covering the pages completely.

If you don't feel comfortable with creating details like the moon, stars and the sun, leave the details off and skip steps 4 through 7 and 9. It will still look really cool. You can also sketch simpler designs and use those instead.

REFINING THE EDGES

3. Using the rotary tool with 120-grit sanding drum, sand the edges of the book cover smooth. Also sand the edges of the corner decorations, but don't sand the bottom edges. The result of the sanding will look nicest when using a rotary tool, but you can also use regular sandpaper. After the sanding is done, clean the foam pieces by removing all of the dust.

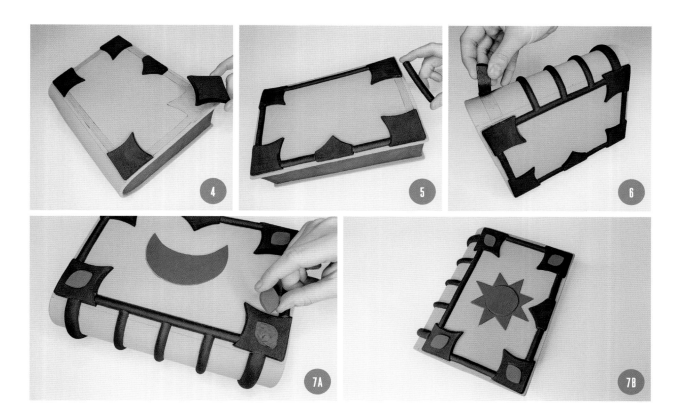

ADDING DETAILS

4. Glue the corner decorations to the book cover. Apply four corners and one side piece on both the front and back of the book.

5. Connect the corner and side decorations with the 10mm half-round EVA foam dowels. Lay them on the book where you want them, and cut the dowel to the correct lengths. Glue them onto the book. Apply glue to the edges where the dowels connect to the corner decorations, so there won't be any gaps between them.

6. Use the wider (15mm wide) half-round foam dowel for the top and bottom details of the spine and three 10mm wide half-round foam dowels for the middle details. Apply contact cement where the spine dowels connect to the dowels on the front and back of the cover, so there won't be any gaps between them.

7. Glue the 2mm-thick eye-shaped details onto the corner decorations.

Glue the moon and sun details to the front and back covers.

Note: The sun consists of two layers.

CREATING TEXTURE

8. Turn on your woodburning tool or soldering iron, and when it's heated up, burn lines into the foam on the side of the book to create a texture that looks like the pages in a book. Press harder to create deeper, thicker lines or gentler for narrower, thinner lines.

9. On the book cover with the sun, use the woodburning tool to burn lines in the foam to resemble sunrays. On the other side of the book, burn star shapes in the foam around the moon.

PRIMING AND PAINTING

10. Prepare the spellbook for priming and painting by heat-sealing. When the foam is cooled down again, apply a flexible primer. Cover the complete spellbook. Use as many coats of primer as needed until you like how the surface looks. I used two layers of HexFlex black. Leave the primer to dry for 2 to 4 hours.

11. Apply a layer of brown acrylic paint to the whole spellbook. This will serve as the shadow color for the blue and gold. Add more paint on the raised parts and less on the edges where shadows naturally occur in order to create some initial depth. If your primer wasn't black, you can also add some black paint on the shadow parts. Leave the brown paint to dry for 2 to 4 hours.

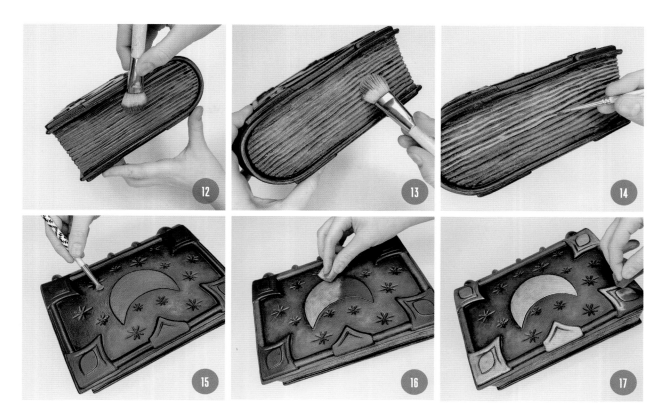

12. Mix a lighter color of brown and apply some paint to the raised areas of the book pages. Only put a little paint on the brush each time and paint in the opposite direction of the lines to make it easier to not get paint inside the burned texture lines. Those lines need to stay as dark as possible to create more depth. Leave the paint to dry for 1 to 2 hours.

13. Mix an even lighter color of brown (almost completely beige) and apply another thin layer of paint on the raised areas of the book pages texture. Leave the paint to dry for 1 to 2 hours.

14. Take the pure beige acrylic color, and with a thin brush, paint on some of the lines to create highlights. Just randomly select "pages" that you want to highlight. You can build up the highlights by adding more layers of this pure beige color so that some of the pages pop even more. Leave the highlight layer of paint to dry for 1 to 2 hours.

15. For the main color of the spellbook, I chose to use blue acrylic paint. Dab it on with a brush to get a nice cover layer of paint and create some instant gradients. Only paint the main parts of the book, and leave the corner details and pages unpainted. Stay away from the corners so the shadow color can still show through. Leave the blue paint to dry for 1 to 2 hours.

16. Apply silver acrylic paint on the moon decoration. (I used Dark Silver from HexFlex.) Dab it on with a sponge to prevent brushstrokes. Acrylic metallic paint usually dries really quickly, so leave it to dry for 1 hour.

17. Apply gold metallic acrylic paint on the corner and side decorations. (I used 14kg Gold from Cospaint.) Dab it on with a sponge to prevent brushstrokes. Only paint the raised surfaces, and not the shadows, to give the golden details more depth. Leave it to dry for 1 hour. Leave the paint job to full dry overnight.

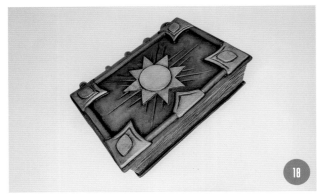

18. Add a layer of varnish to protect it, if you wish. Either spray or paint over the paint with a matte acrylic varnish. I applied one layer with a brush. Leave it to dry overnight.

19. If you want the metallic details to look even more like metal, apply a layer of glossy varnish on the corner details, the sun and the moon with a brush.

RESOURCES AND SUPPLIERS

In this list you'll find my favorite places to get materials. I'm located in Europe, so that's where I source my materials, but since this book is for a worldwide audience, I tried to list suppliers from other continents too.

Of course, this list was made when I wrote the book, so it's possible that by the time you read the book, some shops may have changed their collection. I always advise to check out your local craft shop and ask if they carry EVA foam.

RESOURCES BY PRETZL COSPLAY

More crafting patterns and tutorials on my website
www.joycedesign.nl

More crafting patterns and tutorials in my Etsy shop
www.etsy.com/shop/pretzlcosplay

Crafting tutorial videos on my YouTube channel
https://www.youtube.com/c/pretzlcosplaychannel

More inspiration and tips and tricks on my Instagram page
www.instagram.com/pretzlcosplay

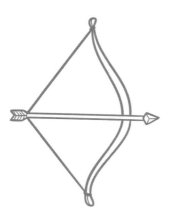

MATERIALS AND TOOLS

Materials like EVA foam, foam clay and prefab foam dowels and bevels

- Minque (The Netherlands) - minque-creative.com
- Cosplayshop Select Style (Belgium) - cosplayshop.be
- Mamike (Switzerland) - mamike.eu
- Craft & Cosplay (France) - cosplay-craft.fr
- Poly-props (United Kingdom) - poly-props.com
- Tyges (United Kingdom) - tyges.co.uk
- Coscraft (United Kingdom) - coscraft.co.uk
- Arda Wigs (Canada) - arda-wigs.com
- Lumin's Workshop (Australia) - luminsworkshop.com
- Worbla New Zealand (New Zealand) - worbla.co.nz
- TNT Cosplay Supply (USA) - tntcosplaysupply.com
- SKS Props (USA) - sksprops.com
- Foamory (USA) - thefoamory.com
- Blick Art Materials (USA) - dickblick.com
- JoAnn (USA) - joann.com
- Michaels (USA) - michaels.com

Tools and basic supplies like acrylic paint and contact cement

- Walmart (USA)
- Home Depot (USA)
- Lowes (USA)
- Amazon (Global)

ACKNOWLEDGMENTS

This book wouldn't have been possible without so many awesome people. I want to thank all these people and many more for believing in me and supporting me during this rollercoaster of a process.

To my partner, Pascal, thank you tremendously for your endless trust in me, for keeping up with me when I was working day and night on this book and for taking things like cooking off my hands so I could keep in the flow of writing. Thank you for the countless pep talks, for feeding me chocolate and cookies and/or making me tea to keep my spirits up and for your overall support to not lose the trust in myself and give up. Thank you too for being my photographer and taking the most gorgeous photographs of the finished costumes so they can illustrate this book so beautifully. I couldn't have done this without your love and support.

To Mom and Dad, for your endless support and believing in me, even when I couldn't believe in myself. Thank you for always respecting my love for fantasy stories and art and for encouraging me to follow my dreams. You are the best parents I could wish for.

To my dear friend Judith, thank you for believing in me and checking in with me so often during the process of writing to keep me sane. You are a rockstar!

To the team at Page Street Publishing, thank you for giving me the chance to make this dream of mine come true. Thank you for creating the most beautiful layout and design for the book, and for checking way too many pages for spelling and grammar mistakes. I'm not a native English speaker after all, so this must have been a chore.

A special mention to my editor, Alexandra Murphy, for keeping up with my seemingly endless emails and questions, for being the kindest person to work with and for your patience and understanding when I needed it the most to finish the work.

To all of my followers on social media and the lovely people I meet at conventions, who all were unbelievably positive and encouraging about this project—you know that you are the reason why I get to do cosplay fulltime, right? And I thank you for it, with all my heart.

And to all the other people I haven't mentioned by name. You know who you are, and that I am so grateful to have your support. Thank you!

ABOUT THE AUTHOR

Joyce van den Goor is the founder and owner of Pretzl, where she creates and sells patterns and tutorials to help other crafters create their own costumes and props. She has guested at pop-culture events around the globe where she held educational lectures about crafting, judged numerous international cosplay competitions and inspired many people to start cosplay for themselves. She truly believes that cosplay is for everyone and does her best to share that vision with the world.

Joyce and her partner, Pascal, live in the rural area of South Limburg in the Netherlands.

You can find Joyce's patterns, tutorials and handmade collection for sale in her Etsy shop, Pretzlcosplay.etsy.com, and on her own website, Joycedesign.nl. You can also find her on Instagram @pretzlcosplay, where she posts a lot of behind-the-scenes content and additional cosplay crafting tips and tricks.

INDEX